THE DRAFT:
THE ILL
SOCIETY

also by Olga Levancuka

Increase Your Confidence in One Day

How to be Selfish
(And other uncomfortable advice)

THE DRAFT:

THE ILL SOCIETY

OLGA LEVANCUKA

Typesetting by *www.wordzworth.com*
Cover Design © Reyl Design Group 2013

ISBN: 978-1-4903-1931-5

For my cosmopolitan family.

"If you cannot get rid of the family skeleton,
you may as well make it dance."
— GEORGE BERNARD SHAW

Contents

Foreword

The Ill Society... Are we really ill? Could you look in the mirror? I dare you. You may be surprised and may even walk away with a smile on your face once you have finished reading this book.

This book is a challenge but in our time poor society, fortunately not a protracted one. The author holds up a mirror to one's society, one's friends, one's family and ultimately one's self. The opinions and ideas presented challenge us and the thoughts, ideas and emotions they evoke could reverberate with you for some time!

The real beauty of this book is that is does not offer a solution. It asks you to look, I mean really look and as stated "Think and think for yourself."

"Once you authentically respect yourself, you plainly cannot humiliate others."

Prepare to remove the shackles and be a true human being; now that would be really freedom, wouldn't it?

Let's start a movement in our own lives ... and pass message on.

—MARIE-ELAINE FRITH
Department of Health

PART 1

Preface

One day you read an article in a magazine, by chance and rather habitually, and discover that you have ADD (Attention Deficit Disorder) or possibly depression; maybe Asperger's syndrome. And in that swift read you can suddenly explain all of the troubles you've been through over the years.

All your excuses seem to now be valid and legitimate. The scope of available illnesses to attach our symptoms to widens and we seem to flourish in the fact that our emotions and struggles can be justified. We cherish the nitty-gritty. We no longer need to struggle to earn understanding when we can proudly display the badge of an excuse. We no longer sense the need to feel odd, or misunderstood – because we are simply ill. It's not our fault.

It may be dyslexia, it may be autism. Or possibly depression, ADD or even ADHD. The pharmaceutical companies are smiling as they have a captive audience.

In fact we are so affected by such new labels, we now take it to a different level. As humans, we spend a considerable amount of time comparing and contrasting. We define ourselves by bench-marking our actions and emotions against those around us.

What feels acceptable and well received by our peers and society as a whole, becomes our guidelines and perimeter. This level of acceptance applies to our suffering too. For example, it has never before been as fashionable to be diagnosed with a mental health issue as now. Asperger's syndrome seems to be very popular choice.

If you perform a simple Google search, you will find a peculiar similarity between the descriptions of Asperger's or ASD (Autism Spectrum Disorder) and eccentricity. Here are the few I spotted:

"Odd, unusual, unnecessary behaviour, maladaptive, clumsy."

We can shape the symptoms to fit. We can interpret the symptoms of the illness to suit our needs.

And do indulge yourself with more thorough research, by all means. After all, here is an easy opportunity to get much-craved attention and recognition without much of the hard work.

Please don't misunderstand; there are plenty of individuals who are seriously ill and require medical assistance and help. I am only referring here to the modern pandemic gathering pace in society of self-diagnosis.

Within our hectic society where we have access to an over-load of information via the worldwide web, we take no time for in-depth inspection or rather honest analysis. If we are handed a rationale we accept it with ease.

As Lars Van Trier says, "I think I have Cancer".

This trend to self-diagnose has gone beyond traditional boundaries and is being applied to excuse our lack of social skills and our relationship skills.

Relationships can be a beauty in disguise and can be a plain pain in the ass. And what a pain it can be. Relationships can trouble us to such an extent that they affect every area of our lives including our wellbeing.

At one point during my psychology course, one of our professors, an English man, suggested during the lecture:

"If you take communication difficulties, social impairment and the inability to look someone straight in the eye as symptoms, well then every single Englishman could be diagnosed with Autism!"

Lucky us! We need to be sure at least four criteria are met before one can be diagnosed with Autism.

What about all the repetitive and stereotypical behaviours? OCD, alcoholism, obsessive jogging, regular cleaning rituals etc… Does make you think, doesn't it? Why not continue behaving like an asshole without any consideration for others? Why not keep getting all the privileges we can at the expense of others? Why suffer alone? We have a pass card for our behaviour, we are ill!

A further example can be provided by referring to the DSM - 1V *(The Diagnostic on Statistical Manual of Mental Disorder of The American Psychiatric Association,* 1994). It cites:

"1. Marked impairment in their ability to initiate or sustain a conversation with others despite adequate speech"

If this was applied to a recent networking event I attended, at least 70 percent of those at the event would fall into this category - maybe even 99 percent before an alcoholic transfusion!

The authorities and the health services have made it easy for us. If you read most of the characteristics of modern mental health descriptions, we are all ill.

Alas, the time we can claim privileges due to our mental health issues are soon to expire, as the demand will exceed the resources.

BECAUSE WE ARE ALL ILL. Our whole society is ill.

The presidents are ill (take former Italian Prime Minister Berlusconi for example: sex addict, or… SEX ADDICT? Erm… repetitive, stereotypical behaviour?). The governments are ill.

The book is without a conclusion. You'll know the answers that are right for you by the time you finish reading. After all, we are all known to perceive information differently. But are we really that different?

Warning

Some of the information I share does not represent my own opinions or beliefs, but the events and thoughts of others that I've been exposed to. Please don't take any personal offence. Read with an open mind and read to the end - and only then form an opinion of your own.

While I am pouring my heart out and sharing some very personal 'behind-closed-doors' information, it may well be that in your childhood you too have been subjected to viewpoints that benefit those who fear others. That may be your parents, your cultural traditions or your teachers. Rather than reacting to it, connect with similar unfair situations where you experienced the same emotions and actions. I am opening my life and sharing the experiences of many, laid out on a table on which you can feast.

I am planning to achieve a butterfly effect here, just like in the chaos theory. As I've been left alone to deal with exposure to different views, I've come to my own realisations about unfair ideas put into my little head when I was young and vulnerable. Now is your time to acknowledge where some ideas you grasped so easily are in fact damaging to your life now. Damaging to our relationships with friends, family and lovers and damaging to our society.

Welcome to our new ILL world…

1

Baby Steps

The symptoms of an illness have to start somewhere.

When I was five years old, I was told that black people are black because they do not use soap. When I didn't believe this, I was bullied into surmise by adults, just because they thought it was funny.

As children, we listen to statements which are not necessarily correct but these can stay in our minds and ultimately affect our actions. This can then block our social integration later in life.

Children are more often than not moulded by their parents to become the perfect image of what their parents failed to become. Usually this is not even an ideal image of the parents themselves, but their grandparents or worse yet, friends of their parents. This is compensating for the social masque their parents failed to create themselves. Out of fear or maybe even respect.

By 12 years of age, I had excelled in many areas - singing, dancing, playing the piano and was requested to perform all the time. Just like the mothers on the sidelines of a beauty pageant, training their daughters like dogs painted as dolls. The pressure is on their daughters to win, draining the enjoyment and tears fall behind the scenes.

I used to sing and was often told to perform a solo, singing in front of the stadium during openings of important events, until my voice broke through overuse and abuse. So then I moved on to the orchestra and so it went on, until I finally found a legitimate excuse to leave. I was beginning to form the strength to speak out in small doses.

There was an expectation that I would become a theatre performer, as I was good at reading the famous Soviet poet Mayakovsky. That was until I chose to read Mr M the way I wanted to. I felt he was way too hilarious and pompous, and desperate for a breath of fresh air - he needed to loosen up a bit. Although, later I discovered he was loose indeed, choosing to live Ménage à trois shortly before he was found shot! Think of a Soviet male equivalent to Marilyn Monroe. Naturally, the official version reported that he 'shot himself'. It could never really be any other way. Not in Russia.

My school at the time had visions of me becoming a prize-winning mathematician, yet I had started to use my voice and had become brave enough to exercise my rights and say no.

By 14 years of age I hardly had time to read, sleep, have fun; in fact I had no time at all for activities other than those which would bring me money or work towards my future. I had discovered my ability to make money and build a world of my own which wasn't controlled by my parents.

I had become an adult way before my siblings and not out of necessity. Alas, it suited me. My parents worked long hours shouldering big responsibilities and by the time they got home, they'd be drained and over-strained, with nerves like needles.

Did I say needles? More like a whole arsenal of high explosives. Guaranteed. Every day and every second of their lives.

We represented the image of the perfect family, regular activities on weekends, visiting the seaside and camping at the river. We were a classic respectable family.

At one stage my dad was taken away from us for quite a few years and then he came back from his lock-up.

I wasn't happy before and with his return I was unhappier still. He had somewhat improved on his Roman beliefs of absolute power.

Besides, I'd been working without my parent's knowledge since I was eleven years old. Until the day I got caught, I tried to keep up my 'good girl' standards which gave me no spare time at all.

I liked this for two reasons.

Firstly I loved socialising, yet many activities with my friends seemed nonsense and time-wasting opportunities. This can best be compared to the ostentation of peacocks displaying their feathers.

Secondly, I was driven by fear; the fear of becoming the classic female, used by her husband as an unpaid slave and then discarded at the first opportunity for a younger or updated model. My dad worked hard to instill this fear in me too. Little did he know that the neighbour's daughters' marriages, or to be precise their multiple failures, gave me more fear than my dad ever could.

It possibly even simply reconfirmed what he has kept telling me for years.

My dad made it clear that was difficult to make him proud and yet I should make him proud - because his child is the best. In fact, anything my dad possesses is the best according to him. Sadly, it took me many years to realise he'll never ever be proud of me whatever I do, produce or become.

Luckily, I gave up trying.

Paradoxically, his brutal parenting skills were the best way to prepare me for life. The humiliations and sufferings I've been through in life are nothing next to what I've been through during my tender sweet childhood.

The death of my husband was the only event which took me off course for a few years.

I was regularly shamed and psychologically abused if I did not meet the standards required by my parents and especially dad. Later the school joined in.

Being a talented child is or at least was a prized possession for a school and (as I've learned lately from my clients) the only way to compensate for their own fears. Fear of being a failure as a correct parent first of all. Fear of not keeping up to the requested or set standards. Fear of being a good parent comes second. My case is far from unique; to this day I meet teens and adults who complain how they struggle to meet their parents' requisites.

One of my clients one day exploded. "How I wish I'd had the courage to do what I wanted to 20 years ago, instead of what my self-obsessed manipulative mother made me do."

My partner's son was dealing with a similar issue and possibly still does. It could be your children are dealing with the same symptoms right now. Or not... You of course are perfect!

Adolescence

Once I reached adolescence, society's norms burst in. The shopping list went like this:

- Get married
- As a female, sex is not about enjoyment
- As a female, sex is a marital obligation
- Climb the career ladder
- Note: every single guy is after me to have sex

Sadly for me and to justify my dad's beliefs, guys were all over me and I'd borrow the explanation successfully.

In fact I used the explanation to the best of my ability to play a game. Equipped with this knowledge I agreed to get married, to take the pressure off and keep other men at bay.

How wrong I was. Apparently once you're married the NEW norm kicks in!

The amount of men encouraging me to divorce my husband was amazing, and this did not decline until I lost confidence in myself.

Confidence is way underrated.

Confidence and charisma drives people to be around you and to be part of anything you do. Not beauty, as many believe.

And finally, when I became an adult, I've been told and still am:

"You can't."

"That's not how it's done."

"No."

"Why do you do that, there is no point."

"You are not allowed."

"You can't."

"You shouldn't."

"You mustn't."

"You can't."

On a very very regular basis.

Am I disturbed? Are my parents tormentors? Are you anxious about something? Are your parents making you feel guilty? Are other parents mentally sick? Are others confused? Or are we all simply and blatantly ill?

Every single one of us.

Or maybe, just maybe, the generations of our overly protective ancestors had so many deep-rooted fears that in order to survive they helped us to build our psychiatric asylums brick by brick?

And it is possible that with years and years of managing to sustain our fears, we have built prisons. Not for our fears, but prisons to keep ourselves safe from fear. Only by doing this, we fail to recognise that fear has a purpose.

2

The Mental Health Chapter

When I went for a meeting at the Department of Health in London, my attention was seized by a rather loud poster asserting:

"WE ALL HAVE A MENTAL HEALTH PROBLEM"

Who am I to argue with the Department of Health? The poster went on stating: "Even if you haven't experienced a mental health problem yourself, you almost certainly know many people who have."

I'm not sure about you and your friends but the majority of Americans I've met or spoken to are or have at some point in their lives been on anti-depressant drugs. That means they have or had a depressive illness, right?

Other conversationalists from varying geographic regions and parts of the world weren't as open as my American friends, yet something tells me they're not the only ones.

For those not taking anti-depressants or owning up to taking them it seems alternative crutches hold them up, stabilize or enhance their moods. This might be alcoholic lubricants, fatty foods, spiritual journeys, obsessive jogging or even non-stop reading. Society as a whole is becoming a junkie, hooked on alternative therapies.

We've become so disillusioned and brainwashed with rules, standards, laws, religious schools, movements, churches, equality, rights laws, social norms, family obligations, parents' instructions, advertising, media influence, TV propaganda, statistic results, medical discoveries and religious dogmas, that we can no longer decipher what we want to feel.

We listen to the voices of our relatives, friends and all that they do whether we are aware or not.

Each source in turn brings its own rules, standards and what's good/what's bad norms. Instead of acknowledging that we are lost in a web of disconnected and contradictory laws, we think that something is wrong with us. We never question authority nor established beliefs.

If we still suspect we are ok but we don't understand the 'rules' then our relatives or friends think that something is wrong with us, because we do not follow what they think is correct.

We refuse to be honest with ourselves. We are desperate to follow some sort of system to establish the 'goodness' of our heart compared to the average Joe.

We want social recognition and reassurance, so much so we substitute our true spiritual desires with the sightless following of religions we do not understand. As long as we can be provided with another penitentiary with any sort of confined, abused and cyclical patterns, we can sustain our systematic approach to life… crawling, worm like, digging deeper.

If at this point you insist that this book is not for you, I beg to differ.

It is precisely for those of us who have crawled our way out and see our potential and uniqueness.

This book is for the single, unique warrior looking to survive the swamp, not wanting to be swallowed up as you navigate your way, sometimes blindfolded or not able to see clearly. You can be as excellent as one can be, and yet you can still be defeated if you're not aware of how to wade or walk through the swamp without getting swallowed up and consumed by it.

Those who crawl out are simply happy to be. For we lack an understanding of humanity, purpose and our core reason of existence.

This book is for those who are successful and appear to be happy.

You may honestly believe you ARE happy. The prison you have constructed is so perfectly pre-constructed by your ancestors that the bars have become invisible and you are completely unaware of the constraints of the bars that surround you.

In this book I'll simply uncover the areas in need of our urgent attention just enough for us to never come back to join the army of the 'living dead'.

And possibly even strong enough to bring some of the 'dead' to life, providing our examples will provide them with the pledge they crave.

After all if it's not about a healthy and correct you, it is probably about your neighbours, your partner, your child, your parents - or feel free to make your own choice. I shall humbly join in.

> *"And why beholdest thou the mote that is in thy brother's eye, but considerest not the beam that is in thine own eye?"*
>
> — KING JAMES BIBLE (CAMBRIDGE EDITION)

For centuries we were building our own prisons in our own minds and with all the power we could use, the influence, wealth and or manipulation we were working hard to instill those prisons inside our brains.

We are a scared society. We are ill. We are dissolute. We lack the power to break our own prisons. The first walls and bars of our prisons were built by the ancestors of our ancestors and so on, until one day we have learned how to sustain the blockade. Our mind is not of our own but connected.

Few are trying to shake the bars but possibly their walls have trembled or rotted enough to open out onto new views to the unprepared but curious eye.

Possibly because society has started crumble in its own prison or perhaps purely due to the lack of effort to sustain the barricade. Further more it may even be the weakness of minds imprisoned for so long they no longer know how to keep the bars up.

For whatever reason the destruction is a new event for many of us as we only know what our parents and generations before have told us. We cannot possibly know what our previous ancestors from the multiple family trees have said.

But the habit stays.

When there is a system and we know what we are up against, we get used to the imprisonment. If the walls slowly deteriorate and expose us to the truth we were not prepared to listen, and new opportunities are not tested, we face new fears and new challenges.

We fear more.

When we know we are imprisoned we know we want freedom. It is when we are free we rarely know what we want. And so we create new prisons. By ourselves. For ourselves. 9 to 5. 8 to 8.

Some possibly try to find an opportunity for 6 to midnight. So that by the time they reach home the 'free' family structure does not need to burden you with the social skills you did not acquire in your former prison. Social skills? Did I really mention that?

It is the new world and it is it time to wake up.
More importantly it is time to evolve.

In this book I am not interested in motivating you to do anything. If you read it, chances are you will be motivating many people yourself already. Besides, there's plenty of clever and dare I say bullshit "quality" stuff said and re-said and repeated by multiple cooing presenters and experts who lack knowledge and imagination as well as personal skills.

They appear to be shit scared to try anything new and unfamiliar by themselves. I see them like autumn leaves who no longer shake in the wind but have already fallen to the ground, rotting among other folk who know less then you. They probably have less than you, experience and wealthwise.

I am here to state the fact that we are getting nose to nose with the new changes entering our lives too fast. Technological changes or shall I say implementations. Social changes. Cultural changes. 'Way of life' changes. 'The supply of new information' changes. We are plainly not used to that. We were not taught how to deal with that. We were not prepared for that.

In addition our lack of self-trust and confidence and instilled habit that we have to have a tutor or a guide of some sort puts us under pressure. We try to seek advice from people who are more likely than not even less prepared for such fast evolution of our society and/or ever changing-adjusting-never-stopping lifestyles.

It took hundred if not thousands of years to legalize women's rights and it took only decades to start legalizing gay marriage. It took centuries before the first phone was created and it took decades to create a mobile phone and even less the very first iphone and other technological wonders.

The time has come to acknowledge our state. We are overloaded, over-anxious and over-confused.

I am simply proclaiming our diagnosis, We, who are now living in semi-collapsed compartments of old prisons. And from time to time we abandon them only to come back at the first opportunity or only to be sucked right back in by the others, decaying in their minds.

Some of us do try to take a moment and to make a sense of what's happening. Some even try visiting retreats or simply take a break, not to do anything, just to release the tension and understand what might be the next best step for them? Some, luckier take time to acknowledge 'what is it I want', 'what's best for me' and compare this with 'what's best for those who are close' (for example the family members).

So there they are, rehabilitated and armed with the clear knowledge of what they seek, what they next best steps are or simply know what they want out of life…

They even start to embark on their 'journey'. Now the relatives, the coworkers, the so-called friends do not always appreciate such changes. Mainly because they have their own fears. For example you decide to start your own business, your parents will do everything possible to stop you because deep inside they do not want to provide for you for the rest of their life. Sure they say they don't want to see you hurt. But you need to remember, it's always about them. Every advice given is always based on their experiences and not yours. Any advice people give you is based on their internal confidence and not yours.

For example you have decided to work towards a promotion in a big company. The job pays well, offers exciting opportunities. Sure you'll see your family less but it supports your main life goal so you decide to go ahead. Not long after you land yourself the job your friends seem less pleased.

Those surrounding you may be happy for you to earn less. They will submit to the pledges of support to your spouse.

Because we did not see the bigger picture, nor negotiate beforehand the time spent with the family will be limited. The fact the money may not even be enough to purchase a new house as the nanny may be brought on board to assist our other halves to deal with the overwhelming new workload of looking after the kids.

Interestingly, family friends will be happy to jump in to save the so-called struggling partner, and usually not out of genuine interests but purely because they hate the fact you earn more. They are jealous, yet on the surface their behaviour is of a Good Samaritan.

The reality sets in, and we want more! Because we did not look ahead, or negotiate beforehand.

While the fault may seem to be obvious, in fact both parties have failed to communicate all pros and cons before jumping into a new commitment. Worse yet, people fail to negotiate their working conditions/contracts when applying for a new job. They get so excited or desperate they forget to see all pluses and minuses the new position may potentially bring in.

The fact you want to implement any changes – that's great! Yet an understanding that the changes will affect those close and dear to you is essential. It will be difficult to embark on any new journey should you fail to negotiate or communicate such changes with those who are close to you. Or in other words you need your support group, should you wish to succeed.

With every one change you make, there will be at least two resistant forces…

How do you juggle?

You don't. More often than not, you collapse under the peer pressure. Hence we abandon our goals, only to come back at the first opportunity or only to be sucked right back in by the others.

Society is ill.

Society is ill mentally.

Society's many members are disintegrating.

Are you one of them?

How do you know?

Why do you want to know?

With any vague hint of threat we retreat to our cells, we shut down from the rest of the world. We block out any communication and we efface our true state with any material possession we can acquire, borrow, steal or put on a credit card.

We are getting so scared of everything, everyone and any possible changes that it is almost as though half of the planet's sole purpose is now to fight continuously for stability and security, at all costs. No wonder it feels like so many people's key purpose is to breed an army of public servants.

Especially the type of servant dreaming up new rules, laws, regulations, constitutions and instructions. All of them categorically directed at preventing any change in an already corroded and corrupted society. Didn't Greece teach us anything?

It's either that or the rest of us, who plainly and bluntly DO NOT CARE. In that sense we are all at the latest stage of endemism.

Although it sounds dramatic, the next stage on the degenerative path is to become an endangered species. After that, the last stage is death or as scientists kindly describe it; extinction.

Before I switch swiftly back to us, a note on our governments, the governments we choose (or we choose to believe we choose.)

Our governments and presidents are just like us. And while I don't remember who said first that each country deserves the ruler it has, I still find it amusing that an Italian lady might be upset with my earlier comment on Berlusconi.

Italy - a passionate population full of pride. Italians are known for, or at least the stereotype suggests, being very inflexible to change. They are also famous for their insatiable sexual appetites – hence Berlusconi's example.

If you believe that other countries are more united, isn't England topping the scales for having the highest rate of single people living alone? What, not anymore?

The other day I was reading an article in *The Economist* on Japan and their government, where it was shown that even after the famous 2011 triple disaster – earthquake, tsunami and nuclear meltdown, the ministries put their own interests ahead of the victims. But while the Japanese people's trust in national institutions has plummeted, their hierarchy structure remains, because their class/level submission is unquestionable to those in authority. Always has been. That's in their history.

They have been scared to question those in authority for so long, they got disconnected to such a level that the authorities may well be genuinely unaware of the bigger issues. No one dared to present these issues to the authorities.

Hence, everyone gets disconnected. Everyone is scared or could not care less. Someone had to start communicating and build the social link. Way before the disaster hit.

People will always try to follow old traditions and bureaucracy no matter how outdated and impractical that may be. On the other hand, who works for the government? Mainly people who want stable jobs, who do not want to face any uncertainty. The majority do not want to go through any changes. The only changes people are barely considering are the ones that are promising to bring even more stability, certainty and security.

If we just pause here for a second. Basically at first people want to live quietly, getting by as well as they can, avoiding the hassle at all costs of voting or sharing their opinion with the government. Almost treating the government as another autonomous living thing. Then the change comes, and what? Oh, now you decide the government should be responsible? The government you are barely even interested in? Or as in Japan and some other countries you possibly would not even dare to question?

No one wants to be disturbed. No one wants to argue, especially with the authorities. We do not treat each other as another fellow human being. We first examine artificially created social hierarchy, then we double check with our fears, then we go back to our caves.

If our government executes an initiative against our wishes, we complain. Quietly. What kind of democracy is that? The democracy and communication has to start somewhere.

We are not living alone. We are humans. At worst, we are social animals. That's S-O-C-I-A-L.

Possibly it's about time we really became social, to face and understand the *modern challenges*. Not the challenges faced by our grandparents and other ancestors BUT THOSE OF OUR TIME?

Partially, our communication is placed in our own meta-phorical straight jacket. Partially because our ancestors have created social/governmental/class hierarchy that is not even relevant to our modern life yet we stick through tradition and habit to it like glued and entangled lunatics. If it ain't broke don't fix it?

It is BIGGER – MUCH BIGGER.

We know the world is not still. We know we evolve. Any dogma, any knowledge is only valid for approximately seven years, after that the evolution takes over.

The rules need to be adjusted. The politicians need to adjust. We need to adjust.

I recently read some letters to the editor of TLS and one letter has re-accentuated what I am trying to explain here about the changes/communication and new type of democracy. Here it is:

"Sir, - I apologize that this is rather belated, but isn't it time we stopped measuring historical figures against contemporary concepts of behaviour (Letters, July 7 and 13)? Macedonian society in Alexander the Great's time appears to have been a culture that revered hunting, warfare and other violent pastimes, and to view Alexander as a psychopath because his actions (and those of many of his companions) would be abhorrent to society today and can only be understood in terms of his being mentally ill seems to me wholly anachronistic…

I always think Will Cuppy summed it up best in his short sketch of Alexander:

"Just what this distressing young man thought he was doing, and why, I really can't say". Frazer St John Atkins

It's the same now! We analyze our ancestors and justify our contemporary actions based on the old dogmas that are frankly no longer valid.

Why do WE not want to change?

So what of England… When riots erupted in the same year as the natural disaster events in Japan, shop owners in East London were the ones to frighten off the riots and not the police! Because the government was not only unprepared for the riots, but it is the government which has given birth to over-entitled thugs. The British have a government who failed to communicate that human rights are great and good. But what about the human rights of those who were getting attacked and using any power they can in self-defense?

The fact we are scared means, the government is scared. It's scared of its own people, scared of international laws, scared to lose face in the world of politics, even if it meant fixing some economic and political issues. Fear is the biggest mental illness of contemporary society and its governments. Any fear.

England is a great country (minus the colonial-guilt feeling they'll probably keep in their system for as long as modern Germans will be blamed for the unrelated actions of Hitler).

The English government does everything possible to support poor and uneducated people to stay at home. Yes, you heard me right – stay at home. No pressure is put on them to find work, no pressure to educate themselves. It's more appealing to stay at home. Paradoxically, free courses and free support is in abundance in the UK. I doubt I've seen any other country giving so much for free should you wish to take control of your life.

While England does a lot for education, the bureaucracy and the system is still not challenged. Partly because a section of society - the homeless and jobless - are never going to challenge them.

Sadly, most of the unemployed have enough free or low cost drugs to keep their brain power deteriorating and won't interfere with lives of others apart from demanding even more money from a government facing a growing debt. I mean any drugs here, the legal ones including antidepressants too.

I guess, at least we can call the English government more humane in their way of achieving their mysterious targets. The Russians are definitely more focused on their economic goals rather then the human way of achieving them. Did you know they are trying to make the population pay for basic education with only a few subjects accessible for free? And we are not talking about chemistry or physics classes here, but physical education and subjects the like.

"The only thing a child can get for free - a few basic items. We are talking about the Russian language (2 hours per week), English (2 hours per week), mathematics (2 hours per week), physical training (2 hours per week) and history (1 hour per week)."

I seriously wonder what on earth the Russian government is trying to achieve? A large part of the population is well below the poverty line.

So can we all stop making jokes about Ukrainian hookers and cleaners and other ex-Russians, ex-Eastern Europeans, Philippine maids and so on – some of these people can only think of survival.

It's no longer time for jokes about the sexual or labor exploitation of seemingly 'developed' countries. It is time to acknowledge we have huge gaps between societies, between countries, between cultures and between societies.

I believe those jokes while they are sometimes true, are very unsupportive of people in need and in search of a 'healthier' society. One side has to start first. And while obviously the immigrants and those living in poverty need to implement changes themselves, those who are in lesser need could help enormously not by giving money but by showing a respect to their fellow human beings. No matter where they come from.

What are we laughing at? Our own ill humanity.

And back to our unemployed, 'free everything' for the poor people of England. I really wonder, do cognitive psychologists really mean nothing?

There are so many suggestions and studies, as well as FREE psychological and counselling help, yet they choose drugs. We all choose drugs. We all just want a pill.

If you are on benefits or even just on income support – you get any medicine for free. The rest is just a game of how well one can persuade a GP regarding one's illness.

I met a guy on Hampstead Heath, who we used to fly kites with. He had bought a book to learn all the side effects of dyslexia. He took an exam so that he could get a computer for free. He was also on benefits, while his brother had relocated to Columbia and they were smuggling drugs into the UK. While I no longer have contact with that person – such information should shock everyone! He was a young, fully capable, Englishman with a good education (he came from a good family) yet we taxpayers pay for him to make even more money.

I mean why is the government reaction so slow? Who works for the government? And even those who work and have a decent passion will be soon happy just to get by, as a part of the whole bureaucracy structure and feel lucky if they get to head home on time. One of my former clients who works for the government simply stated:

"I can no longer handle the politics of our directors. It seems as though it is not about the work itself but simply adjusting to the tastes of whoever is next in power."

Do you know where she works? She holds a key government position I don't even dare to disclose! If she can't handle the environment, what about mere mortals? We do not even know where to start to complain and how to take our needs to the right ears. So how can we all decide what would be best for the whole community, the whole city, the whole country. The whole world for what matter?

And the best part is… While everyone around the world is unhappy with their government or openly bitches about central cities and the activity of the banks (especially in the countryside - country folks loooove complaining about central organisa- tions' wrongdoings. From the comfort of their own sofa of course.) –everyone knows they still depend on them. Really.

A population of disenchanted folk sitting in front of the TV cursing our governments. They don't take it outside of their apartment though. They don't write a letter, they don't state their dissatisfaction. And just like that they expect govern- ments to read their minds…

Everyone has to share the pain and the burden of responsibility.

Starting NOW.

Correction.

Starting centuries ago.

We shouldn't have to wait for another sudden earthquake, tsunami and nuclear meltdown as in Japan in 2011. Or another Russian revolution of 1917 when poor people decided to murder the rich, distribute their wealth and live happily ever after. Where is Russia now?

Precisely.

Taking money away from the rich and distributing it among the poor does not work. The poor do not know what to do with money. Money is a little like vegetables, you need to know how to look after them and how to harvest them, when to save them and when to plant them and when to consume them. But we are not educated about money. Our educational system isn't capable of that. Partially it is inconvenient to educate the masses about money! Those few who are in control, yes you guessed it right, they are scared to lose that control. They fight hard to stay in control.

In addition, we are taught in majority by the poor. I mean the teachers, who earn pennies. Some are sufficiently rewarded, but these are the minority. They usually struggle to pay their own bills, hence their dislike for those who are luckier or richer transfers into their student's minds.

The poor are just like majority of us, who have no clue how to be with money. Who live from one salary to another. Money requires a knack. Money requires an understanding and an appreciation.

Money requires your own self-education and self-control. We do not have self-control. We are addicts. We are ill. We want a constant 'pill' supply. It's the same with money. We want more.

We want more of everything. We won't stop hoarding. Be that hoarding of designer bags, be that hoarding of mountain bike trails, be that hoarding of jogging hours. But hoard we will. We will hoard our habits too. We do not want to change.

When will it become clear that the government and the way the government is structured is no longer serving our needs? We do not need to 'wait for the mood', as one disenchanted civil servant working in Tokyo puts it. He recalls the moment before the end of the Second World War when many Japanese soldiers and civilians realised the generals were leading their country to disaster, but dared not speak out.

However, Japan is not the only country where if people do find a voice, there may yet be hope of revival. Many countries are still like this - especially, and paradoxically the ones like the United States and Great Britain where the immigration rate is higher or least noticeable. Often these immigrant families build a generation of resistance to opposing the government rules that even socially are no longer valid beliefs or established behaviours.

Partially because of an imaginary feeling that they are the secondary class. Partially because of a lack of common knowledge. This may be due to a lack of knowledge about how their new country operates, or due to the ignorance of others and of ourselves. Excuses are countless. Do you know that in London there are Russians who don't speak any English? Just like in old days in Brooklyn? Do you know that we have Polish families who do not speak any English?

Why would you look for a better future in a new place and yet fail to learn about the new place in the first place? Why would you fail to learn about the social structure you want to be part of and then be surprised when you are not welcome? Do you know what is never welcome? Something and someone NEW. The NEW that brings CHANGES. In my understanding of life only ill people who lack social awareness would do such thing, i.e. fail to communicate and fail to socialize.

In the olden days they were kept in mental asylums, not necessarily because they were ill but because society could not understand them. Neither party made any effort to start communication. Well, luckily we are living in modern times and such actions no longer happen. Right?

Those few who dare to challenge the establish rules and try hard to support much-desired changes... what happens to them? More likely then not, they don't withstand the pressure to keep everything at the preferred pace of stillness.

If we do not take care of our countries, nations and politics then we'll simply have to join Mr Steve Hilton, mainly known as Cameron's former Strategy Director, in our constant search for a new easier or better place.

While I do not have an opinion on rightness or wrongness of Mr Hilton's ideas and policy transformations, the fact his frustrations with office where the main reason for departing from Cameron's side should really get our attention. It is usually our inability to voice our needs and consideration for others that leads us to later disappointment in our own government, which we may well not have chosen because we were not interested in voting in the first place.

I can hear some of you commenting "But what about those places where you can't even vote?"

This book is mainly for the residents of countries where we can. If we do show other countries that by stating our voice we can achieve what we seek, they just may follow by example.

But then again, this book is not for those who starve but for those who slowly decline and then find themselves in a position they never expected to be.

We fail to evolve and we are too lazy to care. We are bored. We are tired. We simply do not care. We are exhausted. We've had enough. We are in a rat race. We just want to be happy. At any cost. At any seemingly easy cost. At any cost, providing the results are instantaneous. Pills will do, alcohol will do, sugar will do, sex will do…

This is about the fear of change. Fear of making an effort.

Just a quick example before we move on, to show how we blame people for not achieving what they promise; when in fact we did not give them any support. In our defence, our own laws make it difficult for mere mortals to offer this support. Catch 22 at its finest.

- Mr Hilton's restless zeal to reform the state has come up against bureaucratic inertia, political caution and the constraints of European law in 2012
- Tony Blair was considered a reformer but only managed modest tweaks in education, delayed tackling welfare and left the management of policing alone
- In Japan, after the 2011 tsunami, in rescuing the fishing industry, the first dose of aid went via the fisheries ministry to the trawler men. Icemakers, without whom the catch rots, fell under a different ministry and got nothing
- Mr. Obama… (sigh)
- Albeit the United States was the country everyone was looking up to for change, there seems to be an upsurge in British government to stimulate the social response

There are definitely major moves towards on deregulation, decentralization and shrinking bureaucratic bodies in the UK. And these efforts may well be successful if we all wake up.

Yet the opportunities for the UK residents are feasible chiefly due to the fact that any changes in the USA come with an enormous time lag, as the region is so geographically vast.

Russia is probably a long way behind when it comes to fast modernization, due to its size and various aspects of the culture and government. Out of all the countries in the world, Russia's course may be longer and less linear.

On the other hand of course the changes welcomed by other countries (China in particular) may push Russia to make economic and political ties with the United States - that in turn would support or implement some changes faster for both countries. That is of course if Russia has no choice but to combine forces with its long term 'frenemy' in order to unite against the growing virtue of Asia, or what Sotheby's art department lovingly call 'Chindia'.

• • •

Let's look at the modern causes of our mental state. Let's look in more details. What are we up against? What barriers and what prisons that I am so generously referring to? Let's touch on the situation in developed countries with a great welfare system in place.

If anything it is probably the most bizarre element of the Benefits Agency which makes sure that people sit on benefits rather than work. It is long accepted that the average freshly graduated couple will slave away in order to meet their rent payments while paying for food and taxes; meanwhile some families who have never paid a single national insurance contribution will continue living on a full state expenses with a strong belief of entitlement to FREE EVERYTHING – FOREVER.

My first husband used to say: "…darling, England is a country for the poor and the super-rich. It's either free or it's really expensive. I'd rather you choose to stay poor here, otherwise you need to pick another destination."

He wasn't far from the truth. The UK state system has a major impact on struggling middle class, especially in London where costs are significantly higher.

Soon after he first mentioned this, I found the proof.

One day during my lingerie time (I owned a lingerie company), one of my contractors came in distressed and hurriedly informed me that she needed to shorten our meeting as her boyfriend had just lost another employee. The employee was earning approximately 21k a year, back then in 2003.

The employee had calculated that it was cheaper for her to quit the job and claim benefits, since she had a child. My contractor's boyfriend got so distressed that his partner offered her own help. It took him time to find a substitute and he almost had to shut his business. The very business which provided people with jobs and salaries and brought growth for the UK economy. The economy that in turn supports everything or nothing - you either slave away or you stay poor and we pay for everything.

The anomaly is among people who don't want to stay on benefits. I have happened to work with a girl as a part of my voluntary support who has a small child. She plainly had to run away from her abusive husband in the middle of the night with no things on her and a baby that was only months old.

While charities and numerous organizations have succeeded in providing her with very much needed support and legal aid, the financial side obviously was passed to the Benefits Agency. She did get great help.

It wasn't easy and she fought for this help for almost two years using all the support financially and emotionally her friends could give her. At the end, half on the verge of mental illness and half starved she got free accommodation, free nursery school and most importantly, free courses for her to acquire new skills so that she can work. Great, right?

But then there was a dilemma. That girl with the copious amounts of internal strength collapsed. She came to me crying and mortified. She wanted to work part-time as the £50 or so she was getting in cash a week wasn't enough for food and other necessities for both of them. The double bind was however that if she worked part time she would lose most of her benefits maybe even all of them, and as a result she'd only gain an extra ... wait for it... SIX POUNDS a month.

Either the social security and benefits system is way too complicated for our brains, or the government secretly wants us to become more stupid and more useless. Either that, or the people in charge are detached from real life.

I don't think so. Yet it does not add to the UK's government reputation, and it seemingly wants to join the other governments whose reputation is definitely in tatters. Along with everyone getting acrimonious lately.

Let's have an overlook at our current society worldwide.

We are now divided by culture, race, sex, body weight, physical abilities, age, class system, wealth, power, job, hair colour even; just to name the few.

The British publication the *Daily Mail* stated in one of their articles: "Too old for a two-piece? 39 is the age at which women should give up bikinis for good..." I beg your pardon? Are we now divided by the way our body looks vs age? What about 19 year olds whose bodies have never seen better days? What about man boobs? What about..?

Can we force male joggers to wear man-bras? Should we also give out free ball pouches to the aging executives with shaved heads who feel as though they are 20 years old while clearly past 50, and still wearing shorts that display them in all their glory during stretching exercises? Do we make the 18 year old girls wear tights when they follow the new shorts fashion, because frankly their cellulite is spreading way faster than mum's did?

Every culture is different, every race is different, every sex is different, every country now is different ... what's next? No, really?

Which side do we stick to? Which traits do we keep and which ones do we abolish and never touch again?

Do we pretend to sustain our social status by leaving emotions to the poor people, as in England? Do we cover our cowardice by being smiley hypocrites, replying yes to anything like in Thailand and India and keep the grudge inside till we manage to get together with others to avenge the offender? Because we are cowards at heart and can't do one-on-one. We do not want to learn to improve our communication skills. We just want the world to be the way we, with our egos want.

Do we perform as in Japan and in high society so ferociously protected by the upper classes of London or the desperate housewives of wealthy Greeks? Do we behave as ignorant as many Americans who know no other world exists apart from United States?

Do we just say it to your face, like the Russians who can hardly sustain their temper and deal with everything in extreme measures? And pray that their dinner party is not going to end up with a good fight among friends and a broken nose?

Do we behave as loudly as the Spanish and simply refuse to shut up even if the conversation is useless?

Do we continue feeling respect for our own country yet know we are second to Brits should we come from Australia, historically (and obviously no longer correctly) referred to as the land of whores and thieves?

Or should we slightly stay aside as Scandinavians do?

What's next?

For once if you read this book, you are neither poor, nor really poor since you can read and you can afford to purchase the book or… your parents have given you an upbringing where a good education as well as reading books stands for the compensation of your currently-inherited identity. Hence you understand exactly what I mean in such an uncomfortable verbal explosion.

Long before my Greek husband has passed away he said "Olga, if anything ever happens to me, promise me never to go out with or date Australians or Indians.

They have this 'second sort' complex that will drag you down. It's history. It's hard to explain, it's in their brain." In answer to my question - why do I not feel the same complex? He said "You are white and you are a Russian who is an academic."

I mean really?

We are that prehistoric?

We use no common sense to live a modern life and progress and evolve socially. We feel the need to drag our heritage along as well. The heritage that we did not earn if I may remind you - our ancestors did, not us. What is the purpose in trying to protect our own imaginary safety nets? They are no longer working for the benefit of our human race. In fact I doubt they work even for us. Rather than welcoming new opportunities and living life, the force we drive is directed towards seclusion and isolation.

It is really sad that with all the progress in communication and social life, as well as the speed of exchange of information we DO NOT WANT TO LET GO.

We do not want to let go of old, no longer valid prejudices.

Later in my relationship with an English gentlemen from the famous Sainsbury family, I asked "Why do your hypocritical friends speak highly of this guy and yet trying to diminish the other guy when both seemingly come from a similar background commonly known as lower class?"

He replied simply "He is an academic, once you are an academic the class system does not apply. It's as respected as the upper class." I mean, for real? Why? What leads us to believe that because someone has a degree or a high position or a pedigree heritage – they are cleverer or better than anyone else?

So many dramas and super-complex web structures of society are still in power nowadays and if you think you are above all that, think again. There is a meaning in saying "You can afford not to care."

If you think I am a horrible mean person, you are wrong. I am as much of a hypocrite as you are. Why do I have the right to say such horrible things? Because the stereotypes are still very much alive whether you want to agree or shut your eyelids very tight and lubricate your throat with some fine wine (which I still don't quite get the hang of by the way, although I am madly in love with Coche Dury, should you wish to get me a present).

If that's not you then you most likely give some money to charity (to avoid paying taxes, or out of the goodness of your heart?) and pretend you are a good citizen. Or you participate in charity support or voluntary work.

Possibly jogging or participating in triathlons.

While many honestly believe in the cause, let me just help you to overcome your precious moments of feeling good about yourself.

Just get over it.

If you shout about the fact you've given support, then you want people to think well of you. You lack self-esteem, or plainly you lack confidence, for you need to prove to others you are doing something valid and recognisable. And to help you go down the drain faster with your "I am a good citizen for I care." here is another example.

Recently I've been stopped by a friend who asked me and my partner whether we are willing to support his son in a charity Cycle London ride. When my partner smiled and asked "so who is he supporting this time?" the friend, with a smirk on his face (like who cares?) said: "I think to sponsor a rugby game in Rwanda." Both have exchanged knowing looks. He is not the only one.

Many, instead of learning to welcome the new changes and concentrate on catching up with ever-evolving social skills, find it easier to learn to own a social mask. And they live within our structure using this social mask, be that heritage, a good degree or participating in 'approved' social activities to benefit as they can emotionally, physically or otherwise.

Really, if only you knew that information can't be hidden. If only you knew that we know you're lying. We might not even know you're lying, yet something just doesn't feel right, and that alone makes us more cautious towards you. The masks you wear, we wear them too. We really all know, we are just scared to confront each other, because that means we need to acknowledge we are ill with fear, for we wear our masks too.

If only you'd accept that everyone is dealing with life in the only way they can, possibly then you would try to become more compassionate and more sociable. You might try to understand others and possibly share your knowledge with each other, rather than playing a peacock game continuously during your business or social gatherings. Only later to return to your carefully crafted mental cave to replay and re-analyse whether you did your best or whether you could do better at displaying your feathers.

Doesn't it hurt your head to do that? For start, as one TV presenter once said: "Why would you let anyone to live rent free in your head?" And for another reason, you yourself overload your mind. You yourself make yourself ill. You don't go to the gym and continue exercising til your body can no longer handle it?

So why do you do that to your own mind?

No wonder the mind can't handle it. No wonder the mind gets sick. You yourself overload it, with mental social games and artificially created lies and an imaginary status of yours you want to sustain. In fact you may not even realise that those who are around you may just simply like you for who you are without the dazzling web of imaginary protection you mentally knit to be ready for the next social interaction.

If only we learn to be true, with ourselves, for start. Just with ourselves for now. You'd free up so much space of your mind. You'd simply give a little bit of rest – rest your own mind needs.

For example, another friend of mine wanted to participate in the London Marathon. The only way he could run is if he did it to support a charity. Since the charity of his genuine choice had no spare spots left he picked whatever was on offer. The Gorillas' charity. His explanation to me was – "I just wanted to participate in the Marathon, what the fuck do I give about the charity? As long as I get to run." Hilarious how fast he came clean with his real motives this time.

Remember 'the system'? As long as we have *the system* we know and we can choose. Either follow or abuse. Even a lying system. We just keep our mind occupied with one system after another until one day it collapses.

Do you know why I had an urge to write this book? To show you and ME how ill we've become and that there is still something we can and absolutely want to do. Behind our hypocrisy and addictions, be that wine collecting, charity work, jogging, chocolate, drugs, Wagner, reading, food, fashion blogging or what not, you and I are still humans with a grain of goodness and lack of understanding about the way universe operates.

My prison (or as much of it as I could succeed) has collapsed early enough for me to learn to survive on my own.

While I never ever lived on my own until literally a few years ago, and there always was and is someone present to look after and care for and adore me. It's just the way it is for me. I really do not know why.

It is the very fact that I wasn't alone and yet was trying to achieve my own goals against everyone's wishes or without anyone's' moral support that caused so much depression, unhappiness and several suicide attempts. Because everyone cares. From their point of view. Based on their failures. Based on their victories. Why would you try to live someone else's life when you have your own? What is wrong with yours? What's with all this "You should do this." "You are better off if you do it this way." etc. Never before have we had so many advisors and friends. Hang on. What's wrong with your life? Why do you not take care of it? At least take care of yours first.

It is different for me now.

If there is anything in the world I know well, it is human nature. I am not an idiot, I learned early enough that my looks can get me a lot, and I mean a lot. Yet even earlier than that I learned that one day looks may go (though lately I am learning how and why they can stay) and it is your human or social skills that can get you anywhere you want. Not money (though that certainly helps) and believe me, I saw those poor fucks quivering on their knees in front of my 'English gentlemen' boyfriend to make sure he thinks they are his friends, just so that they can keep up their appearance by keeping an affiliation with him.

Possibly partially because I had to learn and to acknowledge that he needs them as much as they need him, to feed his ego. So there I was trying to live his life for him...

And what's wrong with that? That they feed his ego in such a way? We all want to be respected and admired, don't we? Even the hardest bastard who claims to see through people can still melt at a genuine compliment. And that's what you do. That's what I do. At our core as a human being, we have our ego, that is meant to protect our interests at heart. Yet it seems that we definitely haven't got to grips with controlling our own ego.

We learn social skills where and when we can. Usually the easier way, simply picking them up from where those around us have left them. You learn when to distance yourself from someone who doesn't fit with your desired 'identity', when to compliment or when to recognise the competition and do the 'cutting' at all costs.

I am proud enough to have as many good true friends as I have enemies who work hard day and night to ensure their 'cutting' strategies work and I am not appreciated in their social circle. I've now learnt to appreciate that those who don't like or don't agree with me at least (I hope) have something they believe in that is worth preserving. If everyone likes you, then you're probably a struggling Narcissist who is in love with the desired reflection of yourself in the windows of society's eyes.

Never mind my English boyfriend.

When I worked for a Mafia guy, the tricks people would do to get themselves on his good books were beyond what Shakespeare has achieved for the literary world. They were the best forms of manipulation. Dale Carnegie wouldn't simply be proud, he would have hair standing on end at such innovation in human skills.

Dale Carnegie would resign from his job.

While some of them simply wanted to wake up next morning alive and preferably in their beds, the majority simply wanted to get into his good books so they could drop his name and instill fear into their business opponents or simply to impress the girls and possibly get free sex.

The methods are different but the purpose is the same. Agreed? ;)

If you think I am for spilling my society games, you are up for a bitterly disappointment. Well I will spill a little bit. But you are no different. You are as pretentious as most of us are. You fight as hard to sustain that social image, you have or you believe you have, as you can. You grow up with any addictions you can afford in the ever growing complexity of this life. And with any means you can get hold of. With any skills you have or you have mastered.

Almost 50 percent of my first sessions are spent with my clients on identifying the habits, and at times very very costly habits, that no longer work for them before moving onto accomplishing their list of goals.

Yes, the saying 'the good old days' will always be true. For this generation. For the next generation. Hopefully after that we will learn. There are no good old days. This is just not the way our world works, this is not the way the universe is evolving. The rivers are always flowing, one direction or another, but they are flowing.

The saying goes, the best medicine is the one that treats the cause and not the symptoms. However you and I are more familiar with symptoms, hence I shall continue with some symptoms of our social illnesses.

Because, you are the educated crowd, you are the one who is in control (even if this is delusional).

You, the reader, are ok.

You know that no matter what, you'll survive.

You have the skills and you probably have a bit more, either money, family or maybe you are amazingly handsome with a touch of brainpower, or you come from a good 'breed'.

You are the responsible one.

You know that jumping from one addiction, be that yoga, collecting wine, cars or anything in fact – even lovers; be that regular trips to Thailand, attending a mind calming seminar in a countryside, reading every notable novel or just taking up some regular activity classes… it can be exhausting and tiresome yet you do realise that addictions are what keep you alive in the face of your well paid yet mundane job. And with addictions, we should start our next part of the book.

Why addictions? Because in addition to everything else, we are cowards. Yes, this cowardly society is so afraid of everything that is trying to create any possible protection from that constant fear. You may even temporarily forget that you live in fear, work or mundane life chores are taking over, if nothing else works just a drink after the office and a cigarette or a heavier substance will do just that.

I attended a party once where a woman was openly and passionately discussing how she is creating a more female persona in her financial city environment, since she is aware of her masculinity. She has even forced herself to cry when one of her colleagues left as she thought that was what was expected of her behaviour-wise!

As you see for some, addictions can even sustain the social image they believe they *need* to project (unaware of the fact that their behaviour is very unnatural and freaks out a lot of people, making them uneasy in your company).

In addition to these addictions, you are used to society's regulations. And you stick to the rules you know without even suspecting they can be different in other countries. Well, you know they are different but you hide your head in the sand as though you are an ostrich, and hope that all your ignorance somehow will keep you afloat.

At the end we all have addictions, regularities, inflexibility, ignorance, an absolute knowledge of everything and what not - all mixed in, only to add to our already overly confused state. Possibly we think we are not confused, we are surprised.

Yes we simply surprised that the events are not as we expect them...

While some prefer playing more direct theatrical games as in the above example, the majority of you are absolutely comfortable in your office being yourself and sticking to propagating your new yoga classes or your religiously healthy lifestyle and a variety of newly acquired physical activities which make you feel above the rest, or at least it make you feel among your kind of crowd.

You feel as though you know how the world works and you believe wholeheartedly you know exactly what is it has to be done with the Greek economy or suddenly give a major recommendation on how Russian politicians should run their country.

Yet throw you in the middle of the no-go areas of Philadelphia or better else to the favelas of Rio de Janeiro and you will give anything you have or can in order to live.

You'll cry like a baby at the first sign of abuse.

You may try to put up a fight. You see, you have something to lose – they don't. Besides, they are cowards too, hence they'll tie you up in packs and you have no chance of sustaining your dignity, without a bit of luck.

Why go so far away? Throw you in the middle of Moscow without your private chauffeur and your Russian friends or attached 'protection', and should you go to the wrong area or drive the car in a 'correct' way, if not the locals, the police will get you.

If you doubt my statements, I have been personally arrested in one of the top Moscow hotels while accompanying... MY DAD! and working as a translator for an oil company.

Dad and myself had just said goodbye to my dad's Swiss business partner and had entered the elevator to go and pack our bags. The lift was abruptly stopped and the police at once snatched me out of the elevator on the charges of prostitution. I was young. I was very young. Luckily my dad, being a former what we call 'system man', knew how to handle the situation. With his eyes he signaled to me to be calm and keep my mouth shut while he did the talking. Only 30 minutes later and before they even got me to the police station they have gotten the proof from my dad that in fact I was his daughter and if I remember correctly my dad even got an apology.

Only because he had this rare survival instinct and he knew how to speak and when. If not for him, they'd have kept me in a cell overnight trying to get a bribe from my family even though it was clear to them that it was my dad. Gang rape would be another option should I be less lucky.

My English lawyer friends were a bit less lucky. My two friends were stopped on the streets of Moscow with the excuse of checking their identity. The naive 'foreigners' where not educated about the peculiar habits of Russian police, though my close friend was not as naive and suspected the real motives behind it. In fact it still remains a mystery how his friend ended up staying in a cell overnight in a hope of getting a bribe from him, only to be released 24 hours later (that was the allowed time to hold without any charges). Meanwhile my friend avoided the situation and told me that he didn't let his passport out of his hands. Sounds rather unconvincing, but then he is a damn good lawyer and I guess he was a lesser coward than those who stopped him. Or possibly his numerous trips to Asia have educated him of other countries peculiarities. His communication skills are definitely to be admired.

What about some areas of the States and London? Unfortunately I have nothing to say about the United States. Though I got lost several times in the 'no-go' locations, surprisingly, local thugs where very supportive and once I was even been escorted by a homeless guy from downtown LA around midnight. On another occasion a couple of big black guys escorted me out of the area because according to them it wasn't safe there (yes, I got lost again).

Another incident occurred on the Washington metro. I still managed to get away without it getting physical. Danger or no danger, should you posses some basic social and communication skills, you should get out.

Not so in London. After infamous nights' party in Brixton my friends and I were getting into an earlier booked cab as one guy has jumped in and another, his companion, was trying to hold the door semi shut so their friends could reach in time to clean up all our bags and the phones and cash.

None of my verbal skills worked this time (which surprisingly did a lot of good in the United States where I felt more scared and out of control and out of my natural habitual city of London). I panicked and as blood had flowed into my eyes and possibly my face, I grabbed the handle of the cab and start banging the door with all the child-like power that I have in order to loosen the offenders' hand. The guy inside the cab, while trying to get a phone off one of my friends, turned around to the screams of his pal, looked at my face and jumped out and rushed his friend away. He screamed back to my party buddies "take care of your friend, she is proper mental".

What's wrong with them? What's wrong with us? Where did we or our society altogether fail to educate each other the basic social skills?

And why do we treat alcoholism and not violence? Why do we treat kleptomania and not bulling? Why do we treat arachnophobia and not fear of life? I mean those teens trying to steal things they have not earned, they are mentally ill. They fear life. In fact they do not know how to live among majority from our social structure. They are ill. They are ill with violence and fear, they are ill with cowardliness and they are ill with anxiety disorders. They are blatantly suffering from mental health disorders.

And what about me or my friends? I know it's dangerous to react the way I did, but years of 'surviving the attacks' (I travel a lot! and often some places I go happen to be no-go areas) have built-in me those weird reactions which have saved me from an abduction and another time from a rape. I did say I am surrounded by people looking after me, I didn't say I was brought up with a silk-layered fluffy pink super protective lining around me.

Why do I share all those examples? Hardly for your amusement. I want to share the fact that I still think of myself as a coward. A coward in addition to the addictions, ignorance etc…

And you are cowards too.

When the riots broke out in the UK where were most of you? At your houses or work, avoiding the dangerous areas.

Of course violence is not the solution (though Americans keep missing out on that fact, with war after war). Our lack of communication skills on a multiple level and trying to sustain whatever safety and security we've manage to acquire is actually leading us to a very very bad 'full-stop' point.

We overload our minds, instead of directing them towards what we need them to do for us. Schools do not have any basic education on the fact that we need to look after own mind and, yes, we need to be in control of our own mind. The mind is to be used the way it is intended and partially it is there to support our social and human interactions in a *healthy* way.

So what have you actually done to genuinely support your own, first of all, social skills, and how you communicate and share your needs with others? Surely most of us have similar issues.

Where has the empathy gone?

Aren't you tired of having a heated debated about politics in front of the TV and taking it no further than on your friends or your spouse?

Aren't you dear cowards tired? Tired of discussing the weather and fine wine and sending your kids off to boarding schools so that you can continue enjoying your social life?

While dealing with confused emotions you dare not share.

Aren't you tired of keeping your smile in front of the boss and then openly criticising him or her behind their back? This may be due to misunderstanding and miscommunication again as at the end of the day you probably do have plenty of common goals. The least would be to keep the company afloat to keep your salary coming, to keep your addictions fed, to keep your social status. The list is endless. How about starting to recognise each of us as a human being, not a thing, not a property and not a material object.

Laugh all you want, yet while slavery officially has been abolished, you know better than I, you can go to any large corporation's head offices to see the proof for yourself. Slavery has never been abolished, it has changed its name and has changed its ways.

It really is baffling how with all the technological developments and ease of communication and nearly instantaneous information exchange, we recoil back into our slughouses.

It is too much too soon.

We really need to acknowledge it. We were not prepared. We still struggle to accept such lightening-like speed of innovation and change.

And to be fair, who wouldn't?

It is precisely why this is the time that empathy, openness and more understanding towards each other would be the absolute minimum we'd need to implement into our lives. Not to feed our fears with addictions, reclusive lifestyles, using our status as a protection barrier.

It is time, my reader, to become even more social, so you can recognise the same pain is faced by many, the same change implementation process is feared by many.

That empathy alone would reduce the list of patients diagnosed with mental health problems.

Simple empathy and seeing the other points of view.

Not necessarily agreeing as you have your targets and your goals you work towards.

Just accepting that the other person may have valid reasons for their point of view.

Instead we grab any opportunity to NOT LET GO.

Maybe I should introduce a new mental health illness: *Not-letting-go*.

The Majority of so-called 'developed' countries are now splitting with a minority who are what we call the 'struggling middle class'. They hate being called middle class. They want to be the ones on top yet they struggle on the way up. The other minority is the so-called super-rich, who are so entailed in their own games they simply are not aware of the real world anymore.

They are aware, and probably more than the struggling middle class but they do still miss the point.

It really isn't about sharing the money as the poor insist, or lending to them under the interest rate, or supporting charities in order to get the tax-(release?) where the most money goes to sustain, first of all, the large and bureaucratic organisation of the charity and those working for it in administration.

We have the other majority, filled with white trash (again of any skin colour), poor, uneducated and blatantly lazy and arrogant idiots feeling over-entitled FOREVER. Working hard to install the guilt feeling in those who more likely than not WORK THEIR ASS OFF to protect the little they possess!

It is everybody's time to understand the underlying issues of such an ill-structured society and learn that is no longer the socialism, communism, capitalism or whatever it is you want to blame that is responsible.

We are to blame.

We are responsible for such a shitty world structure. We definitely will be from now on if we do NOT LET GO and acknowledge we are a brand new and a very different society.

We are more evolved.

We are more talented.

We are more knowledgeable.

We can now share progress faster.

And so on…

I promise you that people are so much more interesting now than they were previously. People finally (yes, not everywhere) have started to have an opportunity to blossom. To share some of their desires or some of their talents.

Even most teenagers I meet they WANT more responsibilities. They WANT to know and to do more. They want to be equals. And why not?

Why do we not accept that the professors should be challenged once in a while?

Why do we not accept that teachers should be challenged?

Better yet, to educate that certain knowledge is absolutely correct on a certain stage, yet it is no longer valid once we evolve further and the new laws apply?

Why are we so desperate to hold on?

Why does everyone in psychology state Freud was wrong?

How do you know? Did you live back then?

It is very possible that he WAS 100% CORRECT then, it is just no longer valid for our new society.

We are not ill because someone makes us so. We are ill for we fail to LET GO. We are ill for we read books how to approach our relationship issues that are based on the old psychology books rather then simply communicating our issues across and then learning to understand the other side.

We are a modern society, we do not have the problems of our ancestors.

Then why do we do everything possible in our power to follow the rules and fears of our ancestors? Worse yet, we add our daily issues on top of that labyrinth of established rules and dogmas. I am surprised anyone can be called sane nowadays.

We are dreaming of finding other civilizations?

We are dreaming of finding other worlds?

When we, cowards, cannot deal with our own kind? I dare you to wake up. Not just you, the well-off, with a good career, with a home or good family support or with securities of some sort.

It is time to wake up all those lazy leeches we have bred with our idealistic beliefs and have learned only one thing. The world has to feed them and provide for them just because.

Just because they are poor or idiots or both. Just because (aha!) they are clever to make you feel bad and guilty. They use the very emotions on you that you use on your co-workers in order to get what you want. But because you believe you are the smart-ass you fail to notice when you receive your own 'treatment.'

It is time for everyone to be responsible and start dealing with your cowardice. Stop being a smart ass and stating clever ideas to your friends and blaming the government – when it is either you voted for another party or you have not voted at all. As much as you expect the government structure to be less corrupt and more in touch with their people, as much it is your responsibility to state your desires and needs directly to them. Not at your home, behind closed doors like a scared sheep, but in the open for everyone to hear.

It is also time we, who are more fortunate than others, take measures to deal with the poverty and ignorance and educate ourselves first of all about our own illnesses and then we distribute or collaborate with the less fortunate. There is no more time left for anyone who comes to this world to afford to stay a brainless idiot and be a weight on humanity which evolves at such a high speed lately that if we do not pull ourselves together and come up with new solutions and new ideology even if temporary, it is not long left before we wipe ourselves off the face of the earth; in our race of ever-growing greed and power struggles in order to sustain our addictions.

Physical power is the most animal side we have. Yet with that philosophy you won't go far. There'll be always someone stronger.

The mind. The healthy mind is the new and still not fully recognised power you will always possess.

With social media growing at a velocity faster than the fly reproduction rate there is no excuse left for hiding our cowardliness indoors. Now is the time when the concern of the whole world's wellbeing is the responsibility of every single human living on this planet.

And I and you know we can and we will.

I mean, how many of you heard stories that when the September 11th attacks were happening that people fearing for their lives would call their relatives and state how much they hate them?

None? Possibly?

Yet we all know of or at least heard of the stories when people where ringing their families and telling them how much they love them. Because at the core, we are good human beings.

We are lost, confused, anxious, scared, exhausted and possibly overly satisfied yet we are good humans. We want to love and we want to care. We want to be loved and we want others to care.

And what do we do with those who are mentally sick beyond help, or at least beyond help for now? Or what about people with other major disabilities who struggle to be a full active member of society?

A little bit of a side-story to get to the point here.

Before you call me Peter the Great whose famous orders (almost unknown to non-Russians) were to kill any child who is born disabled. And yes I did go to the museum he created, that was preserving some of the disabled children in formaldehyde when I was about six or seven years old and it was a horrifying experience. I believe it is shut now.

What I am trying to say here is that I am not against poor, disabled, ugly or whatever else. In fact I am well known among those who know me as someone who really doesn't care about appearances, though yes occasionally the stereotypes will rush ahead of any intelligent decision and I regret it every time should I take a snap and unfair decision. I am not innocent. I am you. I do have my own demons to deal with as most of you do.

In fact, I did have a friend who once put on so much weight that all my other friends started remarking on how fat she had become, and how it's almost disgusting. At first I ignored such horrible remarks. Later I become angry with my friend for not looking after herself, who unconsciously and clearly unsuspectingly inflicted a 'bad' image on me, and few months later I realised that I am avoiding her at all costs. My friends found it embarrassing to be in her company and started cancelling on our meetings.

After I acknowledged what my subconscious mind was doing I made an effort to see my friend more often. I have never

ever told her about that, yet somehow she got the grips with her weight and she has now lost a significant amount of weight and feels and looks much healthier than ever before.

And she wasn't even on a borderline of what we call disabled, it just shows you how easily we discard a human being out of our lives for not being like us or for dealing with some emotional or physical issues.

More on the topic, the story I care to share next is about the temporary work I've been doing for an Autistic charity. It was probably the first charity where I saw they were genuine. And that helped to accept the fact some charities are not just doing great work, they are much much needed.

All the members in the charity really cared and the charity was run on a shoestring.

The charity produced very impressive work. If Professor Baron-Cohen knew about them, he'd be proud to see their work. You probably recognise the name, for his brother is the famous actor whose movies including *The Dictator* are a sell-out. You might know his equally famous brother among academia circles who's research on Autism is highly respected, if not one of the most progressive.

But here is the twist to the story.

After the training and initial visits to various families and living through their pain I was assigned to a particular family. The family consisted of a single mother with an autistic child. I still respect his mother's bravery and courage and efforts in sustaining her child's life. She fought against a faulty educational system which ignored her child, instead of providing improvement, his condition deteriorated severely and she managed to get funding for his home schooling.

The boy was really good and though it was a heavy case, even I could see his progress. Sounds all happy, right?

Not so.

There is a big moral dilemma.

While, I am quite sure his mum didn't mean to, she kept complaining that she didn't get enough help. I am also sure she was simply exhausted and desperate and everyone who works with extreme cases of severe Autism know how draining the experience of even being near such child for a momentary period of time.

So she had:

A house with a garden,

A special room for the child to study,

A specially equipped toilet for a child,

A car,

1 social worker,

1 cleaner,

1 charity worker,

1 me.

We were not working full time, but each of us had certain amount of hours to do per week, though I suspect one social worker was a full-timer.

She did not get it easy, she fought for it hard, but she got it.

Now you tell me.

Does it make a sense for such a large financial expense most likely from your tax and four healthy people and his mother, to sustain the life of one child?

I know we are humans and we need to care for our own kind, but clearly not at such expense? Yet arguably that child will never ever be able to work and he definitely suffers from his own demons. The whole example is true yet it is something we prefer to keep our eyes shut to.

You see.

You do not even know what's going on in your own country.

If you do, you prefer to defer attention away from things which will make you look BAD in the eyes of others.

Screw you! You fight to sustain your Narcissism when everyone is equally ILL. It's like trying to get out of the hole by digging the hole even deeper.

We have flaws in the system. We even have flaws in the care systems. We have flaws in social-wealth distribution. Yet if we do not stop shutting our eyes to what's out there, and to what we feel uncomfortable about, it will never change. Correction, it will yet somewhat downwards.

At the end we'll all end up ill. Who will care for us then?

What about the so-called healthy people? Where can they get some help when they need some?

Everyone needs help once in a while, not just those who clearly need that.

My friend's uncle who was always so happy and cheerful has completely scared her when one day he broke in tears (thankfully they were just tears and not a heart attack). He said: "I can no longer continue looking after everyone. I am tired to be strong. I feel that now it's me who is ill."

Sad, very sad.

And scary. If that's what awaits all of us for trying to be strong, then no thank you.

We need to acknowledge that not just us, our structures are ill.

For example we complain that UK government gives money to India when their people are reading whole books on how to come to UK and put themselves on income support and get a free house, weekly pay and then bring more relatives and all at YOUR, (the taxpayers) expenses?

Did you know that when USSR broke down, many lied that they were harassed in order to get an asylum seeker status?

Our systems (in any country nowadays) have flaws. At least let's start acknowledging them. Publicly.

Another argument is, you forget the rationale for such money sponsoring and close your eyes to the income support going to the foreigners and foreign countries. You forget your angst that these monies go elsewhere rather than your own pensioners who simply are not educated on survival, because they came from the 'job for life' generation, because the UK government has other interests such as a lack of own resources in the UK.

For the very same reasons as USA has all the war issues?

You guessed rightly, the oil countries.

While there's plenty of research done on how to run your cars on other fuel than oil and other resources have been presented which substitute oil. The USA government (and I bet not just them) do everything possible to keep such discoveries under lock because it is a direct threat to their financial power. The governments are just like you.

We are the government.

The government is scared too.

You get some power and like a child in a tantrum state you do everything possible to keep that power.

At all costs.

Even if it costs you your children, your family, your parents and not impossibly your life.

I am a coward. Not by nature but for our common interests. As you need me, I need you, to take our social structure to the new higher and most importantly EVOLVED level.

And that is just a few of the reasons behind the Mental Health Issues we face these days.

3

Chapter on Sex as Commodity

Sex as commodity. Yes, commodity.

There is a spark in the press that the current generation has a different attitude to sex. It says that we have developed a unique talent for detaching ourselves from sexuality. The point is being made we do not treat sex as something special anymore and we feel free to use it as a commodity. While many of you can agree, as many can disagree.

The years of the sexual revolution are definitely well behind. While before expressing free sexuality would be equal to expressing your freedom, freedom of choice. Nowadays sexual freedom is mainly used to get us what we seek or what we want according to some of the press publications. Or is it so really?

With all the hype in spirituality, soul retreats and take on your inner strengths, paradoxically we threw ourselves to a different extreme. Something we know.

The material world we can see with our eyes and touch with our hands, body or something else.

Thanks to our growing isolation, the minutes we do spend together are now dedicated to proving to others we are better, more special or that there is nothing wrong with us. That we are ok within 'our' social standards.

At one of my birthday parties (I usually celebrate several per month) I've made an arrangement for all my girlfriends to turn up. I've suggested we behave silly and get back to our childhood memories.

We where supposed to eat ice-cream and watch *Beauty and the Beast* in 3D. Needless to say, the opportunity to behave like a kid wasn't taken lightly but only til the ice-cream started filling our tummies. As we were giggling and updating each other on the news, one girl suddenly, and with disbelief has asked me whether I was single. I thought it was hilarious and hurriedly confirmed no, not me.

Then she asked everyone else and there it dawned on me.

As a female, on a contrary to the all new modern changes and implementations, as a woman you are a sad case should you be single, especially if you are somewhat between 18 and 65 years old.

Many of my friends hurriedly reaffirmed to her that they are not single and the only girl who was single at the time, shied away and managed to escape the answer. It was better than an amusement park to watch us all suddenly recoil from a seemingly innocent yet intrusively disapproving question.

I got even more proof the next day when I saw the girl who was questioning us has marked her relationship status on Facebook as 'in a relationship'.

The old mantra that women should be in relationship is still running through a major part of the female blood.

And for some men too.

One of my exes, when I asked him why is he so desperate to seal the deal with me (I couldn't care less at the time) said that he didn't want to look like a failure. He wanted to be sure everyone knew he was capable of relationship and he can attract the one. Mainly because of his mother's bizarre motives not to be mentioned here. Nevertheless. The old dogma, no matter how invalid it is in our modern society, still lives in our system and instills fears of such magnitude that many actions we take are based on an irrational trail of the past.

So what's all that about sex and commodity that the press have been talking about lately?

We do not really much separate anymore the need for the material goods or social approval? When we see something on the supermarket shelves or designer boutiques' hand crafted hangers, we think 'can I have it or not'. If not, we start thinking what can I do to have it? But wasn't it always like that? The matter is even worse if your friend has it. And the same with a partner/husband/wife/boyfriend/girlfriend/etc.

It is very common for me to notice that every time I am in a happy relationship, every single friend of mine is becoming desperate to find 'The One'. The number of marriages I and my sweethearts have sparked are significant.

Only recently a brother of my partner, who everyone thought will never get married, got so wined up with our 'vomanting' (that is romancing and vomit as kindly put by another annoyed but married friend who has a significant lack of tender physical attention in her marriage) that not only after 40+ years of his life he has found a girl within a month or so after seeing us - he even got married to her within… less than 6 months! So desperate he was to get the seal of social approval, he brought his bride and her whole family with the army of photographers to London to celebrate the wedding in front of everyone who is even vaguely related or anyone he ever knew.

Firstly let's acknowledge, neither sex nor relationships are used as a commodity.

Both sex and relationships are treated as a commodity. And the best achievers award here goes to New Yorkers. They've exceeded everyone's standards. They even mate with, have sex with, have relationships with, those who meets their long list of requirements. They have what we humble people use as a shopping list, they took the meaning further. 'The shopping list' stands for everything for NYers, including relationship, sex, even picking their pets and the salad bar they eat from.

Sex on the other hand, is used highly as a commodity to sustain the needs of material nature or to sustain the needs of social nature.

Surprisingly that is not new at all and was throughout our whole history of humanity.

It is plain simple.

If there is a demand – there is a supply. There are guys or women who need sex, there are guys or women who are happy to provide it for an exchange… If before it was about marrying and securing your financial future for your cubs, now it has become about securing your work position or securing your rent or securing your holidays or just an expensive lunch or an overdue bill.

It is quite common for a teen to give a blow job or variety of sexual favours to advance in Hollywood and not only there. Yes, usually males in this instance.

It is also quite common to use sexuality to advance opportunity in other work areas. Having sex with your boss in the hope of a promotion or pay-rise. Sometimes it is not even about a rise but that euphoric feeling of empowerment due to the cord-like attachment to the one in power.

Power is an aphrodisiac. Just as in *The Thick of It* one of the ministers replied to his disapproving colleague:

"Yes, we are in politics for that… and the pussy."

It is just the confusion lies where assumption is automatically towards women whoring themselves and not men. Not so AT ALL! Sales people, and especially men, falsify their single status to ensure favours towards them.

It is very common for men working is sales mentioning aspects which would underline the fact that they are single, to spark the maternal instincts of highly charged and attention-seeking single women.

As one salesman put it:

"The minute I've complained about difficulties about my single life, nurses practically fought over who'll make me a cup of tea. I knew I was in to secure the much needed appointment to increase my sales."

During my recent stay in one of the swankiest hotels in Washington where they even provide you with a gold fish as a pet, should you miss your pet who has stayed behind; a male couple next to me in the swimming pool area had a regular relationship trade-off discussion regarding one guy wanting his male partner to purchase him that necklace he saw the other day for $2000,- while rubbing his shoulders gently.

Sex always has been a commodity; it is only now we start speaking about it that way.

As one of my NY friends put it:

"Look at me! Alleluia to NY girls trading their sexuality as a commodity. If not for my money and position and NY, I'd never get laid!"

He wasn't too bad. He was old and bold. Very old. He was a lot of fun though. Yes agreed not my type and I wouldn't go to bed with him. But then the girls he was referring to would be 25 years oldage! Models looks and all. I wasn't even on his shopping list category!

He said NY has it all. Just do your picking and then do the trading between each other's 'shopping lists'.

Many do not realise they use sex as commodity… Many do not even want to accept that sex has ALWAYS BEEN USED AS A COMMODITY.

That was possibly the only commodity women had and still have in many countries.

Until 1857, a married woman had no right to divorce her husband in England. In some countries it is still the case.

Again in England, until 1882, a married woman's earnings, property or any monetary wealth in fact automatically belonged to her husband. Just recently I was having a tea break between my sessions next to a table with two women, one in her late 50s and one in her early 40s, who were complaining to each other how their husbands were the one taking decision in every aspect of their lives and that modern age didn't change them a bit.

It is only since 1928, in the UK again, that women can finally vote at the same age as men. Not so in other countries. In fact even in Britain, and in the USA and certainly in Russia quite few people still believe that women should stay at home and be what we called an unpaid slave. Better else, as one of my stuck-between-times exes insisted, that I should work, and at the same time to be an 'unpaid slave'.

And by an 'unpaid slave' I refer to the childcare and housework that women still continue to have the main responsibility for. Or as the half-true half-joke goes, 'men who can't afford prostitutes prefer to get married; sex is free and possibly even comes with an extra income'.

It certainly seems so when western elder men get married to a younger eastern female then export them back to their western countries and more often then not they find them jobs too. In fact one of the UK government's decisions to try to implement a law saying you can't get married to a person from another country unless you earn x-amount per year, makes a lot of sense.

I've seen quite few women who got married in a hope of a better life naively, only to find themselves slaving away and being in full responsibility for all the bills and housecare without suspecting their final destiny. Yes, the women can be blamed for their naivety, but do remember, they are more likely to come from a country where women have a very low social status, if any. If a westerner makes a kind advance it seems to be a fairy-tale, they expect it to continue. And wouldn't you?

On the funny side though, I had one client who is high flying in her career and so important that you'd beg her to be your friend, such a power she posses in her smart and surprisingly kind heart. A kind heart was the issue.

I had an issue with that. She came to me to progress in her already impressive career, think TV, celebrities, freebies, good dosh, beautiful people around. She has also stated she would like to touch on dating, as for a few years now she has not succeeded in securing any dates. She has plenty of male

THE ILL SOCIETY

friends and she was very convinced that at least half of them where single and heterosexual just not interested in her.

My client is very pretty. To tell you the truth, the minute I saw her, even before an introduction, her body language said either married for a long time, or desperate for love. She had that peculiar vulnerability about her on a female level. In any case after working with me for a few months she at last started successfully dating. Thus far her success with men has extended beyond her needs or shall we say beyond her moral expectations. She had a business meeting in a Sanderson Hotel, at their bar. Apparently she didn't know that is one of the hottest 'pick up' points in London.

Sadly for her, that didn't prevent me from giggling non-stop.

Still, quite offended, she went on sharing how one guy approached her, during her discussion, and blatantly asked whether she'd be happy to join him in his suite at the Lanesborough hotel. Minutes later after she had sent him away, he came back again and asking whether £1000 and a bottle of Champagne will change her mind. At this point she got completely furious and reassured the guy that neither his looks, nor his money were of interest and besides the offer was far less lucrative than the contract she was discussing with her female companions. Neither his company nor the bottle of cheap Champagne was attractive to her. The story would end here, should the guy not come back again half an hour later and tell her he is willing to negotiate the price and increase his 'offer'.

As she was complaining about it I, sadly for my client, only saw the funny side of it. I said: "You mean that out of the whole bar he went for you?

And you mean that he came back for you three times?!"

I thought she should be very proud of her female charms. On the other hand I honestly had respect for a guy who was not lying but was very upfront about what he wants and what he offers. He simply got the wrong type of girl.

After my customer calmed down a bit and started seeing the funny side, I pushed my case further. I articulated the fact the guy was not playing mind games with her, giving her what she needs and then after getting what he wanted dumping her. She never had that by the way, so it is not at all related. I simply wanted to make my point by explaining that it is fine. Many people treat sex as money. Plain and straightforward commodity. It's been like that for donkey's years!

And why would anyone be blamed, when we as a society via the press, media and other ways of reaching out to everyone else are exposing ourselves to commercial, hypersexual images.

Sex sells.

So it's built in us, we learn from a young age to value our sexuality as a commodity to use to our advantage.

Men or women.

Semi-naked images of beautiful people trying to sell you something are everywhere. The airlines are having battles for a sexier or subtler yet sexy uniform for their personnel. The images of well-built torsos are selling your perfumes, the slender ghost like naked nymphs, sorry, they do wear something it's just see-through, selling you designer clothes.

Forget the designers, the high street dominators like H&M and TopShop including our online favourites like ASOS are long following see-through, semi-naked if not outfits, then advertising campaigns. David Backham is now running half naked for an H&M ad.

Alas as with any commodity, when the demand is high, you might have a really valuable commodity, where little spend gets you a long way.

No wonder so many use sex, as sex-work as an easy alternative to the office job and could even parallel their main daytime job. It is really more about how far each of us is prepared to go, and at what price or at what cost.

A celebrity friend of my client (who is a very famous TV presenter in the UK and even made some noise in the States) asked her whether she knew what specifically he was after (referring to the guy mentioned earlier) When my client has denied it and gave her a look, the presenter half jokingly, half truthfully said "Well if it was a blowjob for like thirty minutes and he'd offer five grand for it, I'd definitely do that!" I am sure that was a joke, and I bet you'd do that for sure ;)

Though our lust for pretty new designer gear may have something to do with it, it is more complex than that.

Yes, we value the ownership of 'stuff' highly, and seemingly more now than ever before, but it is also about power.

Power of giving. While both sides benefit, each part gets to experience the moment of power. The giver – the power of having the much desired commodity, i.e. sex in this case. The receiver – the power of dominating and satisfying the fact he or she can have anything he or she wants, because they've got the dosh or flat or a ticket or an opportunity to advance you in your career...

Both parties win, just there is always one stronger winner, the one who knows they can get that again. In some lucky cases, both parties are winners.

Why?

Because the major health illness we possess is FEAR. FEAR that is routed so deep we no longer know what we are afraid, so we try to compensate by creating an illusion of our power over life in any way we can, be that sex, be that money, be that social status or something else. Take your pick.

Like in the following case, where everything got confused and demand was raised higher, since one party missed out on the opportunity to 'play' with the toy.

While I'll complete the following story from a different angle a little bit later, the first part reflects the subject in question.

I am quite a social person and due to my work people feel particularly open to discuss matters of a private nature with me, which still takes me by surprise.

With men it is more straightforward, while they still prefer to have one perfect partner, the somewhat physical demands of 'I've still got it' put extra pressure towards relief via the vital organ.

In the female case with our nurturing instincts built-in (luckily not for all of us) we need to offload our maternal instincts. This is less of a physical need, more installed by our mothers' understanding of what a 'good' girl does.

And not surprisingly if we do not offload such maternal instincts on someone we feel somewhat defective, failing, imperfect. That in turn influences our confidence as a female. Here we can use sex as the commodity in exchange for feeling needy.

One of the Hampton mums, whose current work is to look after her children and their house as the men work long hours in NY, and whom I've met through a mutual friend, had a different twist to this.

Whilst being married for some time, and trying to win the sensitive attention of her husband who was a very successful financier (he traveled a lot) she first decided to concentrate on her good-wife side. She decided to update their mansion.

It's really common for us to look at some visual proof. Especially if that 'visual' gets approval from your friends and guests.

The interior designer she hired was a darling and slowly started sharing his dreams of future career development with her.

At another time her interior designer started complaining to her he is single. I've got your radars up here, haven't I? By the way, I've met the guy and I was 100 percent convinced he was gay.

As a 'good' girl, our mum was flattered with compliments he gave her. She decided to help him in an exchange for his admiration. First she introduced him to a single friend of hers in the hope of setting them up.

Once that failed and still working on how to help 'the interior designer I adore' she decided to introduce him to a very influential businesswoman who is married. Our mum thought it was a safe bet, the businesswoman was a friend and married. She finally found open arms for her unrequited needs and had sex with the guy.

A week later the guy was shagging away the married owner of a well-known business and our mum got left heartbroken, bitter and jealous.

Unfortunately, it was her jealousy and hurt that brought her to share the tale in not such explicit details with a few trusted friends, as there is no way her husband could find out. He is the main provider after all.

The fact that it was a trade off in the beginning, husband provides, she looks after the house and their kids, did not do any good to her confidence levels. Housework is no longer valued or appreciated since the money have their new and relatively fresh super power over most of the things, people and even nations.

Did you know that Latvia has sold their land for pennies to Americans in exchange for some cash and in order to make it look good with their people they've managed to throw in a new visa agreement?

Did you know that something very similar has happened to Georgia in former USSR? Or China purchasing Paraguay's national natural resources for next to nothing?

Back to our mum. She is not alone. It is very common.

I mean you are bitter, not getting enough attention or sex, you decide to improve your relationship by improving your nest, getting an interior designer who'll listen to you and possibly and more likely than not, extensively touch you.

In fact any serving professions would have to listen attentively to your needs in order to sell their business to you! Take my personal trainer I used to have when temporarily attending an LA Fitness gym.

I possibly even hired him only because based on my observations, he spoke the least to his clients. I forgot the physical stuff though!

LA Fitness trainers are particularly good at the 'hands-on-stretches' routines. The first time I had my that 'hands-on-stretches' routine – I gave such a look to my trainer that towards the end of our package sessions I wasn't getting any of that and had to suffer from pain due to stretching via the usage of weird objects.

Not his hands after all.

And there you are.

Someone is nice to you.

Paid by you to be nice to you.

Still, based on the professional surroundings, you don't take it like that. Besides, they become as 'buddy-buddy' as your hairdressers and it is only a matter of time before you start sharing what's happening at your home with them. With many of 'them'.

One key point worth mentioning regarding self employed professions such as an interior designers, hairdressers, nannies, personal trainers and professions alike – they are out on the field, consecutively improving their social skills with a variety of human beings.

Human beings such as males, females, teens, office workers, celebrities, well-off, middle class, civil servants, cleaners, high achievers, desperate housewives, struggling wannabies… you name it.

While you may be slaving away in front of your computer, catching glimpses of the same faces day after day if you're lucky. While you are fulfilling every need for your children or your partner and they are possibly the only people you see till you go on holidays.

Otherwise for days it could be just your face that you see.

In the mirror.

Yep, that particular interior designer did just that.

After all, one shag with a beautiful mum of three leading to 'FREE SEX' with another desperate, businesswoman who works hard on his behalf to get him more of same – isn't bad at all.

He isn't alone. Many women and men choose their vocation based on what they possibly can get out of it.

I do not mean salary-wise, but whom can one meet and what will one have to do to constantly keep the 'tap' open.

Sex, commodity or something else.

Both sides are going through very sudden changes.

Both parties want changes and they fight against it. Both parties will shut their eyes if that's not what they want and aggressively will push towards what they do want.

It is time to acknowledge that while we've accepted equality between men and women, we fail to acknowledge gender differences such as birth-giving abilities and hence the increased responsibility from one side - as well as our embedded prejudice.

Yes, both parties are only interested in the advantages, while avoiding dealing with the issues. Men and women. Both are alike.

4

Men VS Women?

While it would be factual to name this chapter 'about relationships', for maximum effect, I've separated us into genders: men and women.

You yourself know which side you are more on. Meaning, you can be a male but feel more on a female side and vice versa, you could possibly be a female yet feel more masculine than your female acquaintances.

It is more about pointing out some of the main issues we are dealing with or facing daily in our relationships, rather then being scientifically and anally precise and detached from life; as laboratory conditions from real nature/nurture experiments can show us. The issues that cause us so much heartache and in turn provide us with more opportunities to be diagnosed with mental health issues. Directly or indirectly.

When you are born, you are not alone.

You are surrounded, either with your parents, caretakers or nurses and doctors.

You are born into a relationship or into relationships.

'Relationship' is part of your very existence.

While more and more people are trying to create the balance of sustaining a relationship yet being separate, many anxieties come from misunderstanding how connected and interconnected, as well as dependent on your surroundings you are.

To think that you are in absolute control of your life is as delusional as to state that you are not interested in any type of relationship.

You are born into relationships.

Relationships with others have shaped you. Relationships with the people surrounding you continue to influence you til the day you die. They keep influencing now, as you read this book.

Even your relationship with people who inspire you or entertain you via TV, press and other sources of media influence you.

Yet, with age we learn to separate the relationships we prefer to have, from the relationships we wish to avoid.

I do want to underline here, no one ever wants to be completely alone, but it is true, that some people fail to manage the relationships around them. They avoid a relationship that COULD possibly cause such pain again, if not to avoid any possible relationship at all. Fear of ...?

Fear of multiple issues, even a lack of basic social skills or the understanding that each and everyone of us has his or her own truth and perception, which differs from one to another. It is the very sense of being human, a social being. The fact is, we refuse to be and act social, ie socialise and communicate with others.

While it would make sense to start with you, the fact we are brought up with self-protective habits make us notice similar issues in others while we fail to notice even a grain of the same in ourselves. We are eager to learn about others more so we can practice the opportunity to use them to our advantage with agility.

We are eager to learn about others more so we can practice the art of controlling ourselves. More precisely, this control reaches others, asking what we want them to do for us, for example, be my boyfriend, buy me flowers, be my friend, recommend me to the others etc…

Or at least we'd like to know more about others so that we are able to mould our current relationship to the state we want to reach (without any desire to put a single effort into knowing and understanding ourselves better?!).

Actually that is the same, isn't that?

So we'll take a different approach and start with others. As you wish. Why? It's the less painful path. If it is about you and it hits a nerve, you more likely to shut the book and never come back to it. If on the other hand you find yourself connecting with the information in the previous chapters – you are more likely to follow the case *illustrated* here to the end.

Let me underline again, we are not born to build relationships. We are born into and within relationships. Contrary to what you'd like to believe, networking with those around you, or to be precise relationships with people, are what shapes you. It is better now then later that you acknowledge this fact and learn to control the relationship 'influence' factor (if such a thing is possible at all 100 percent).

At times it is possible and at times not. That depends on many factors at any given time; not within the scope of this book. Yet my task here is only to show you the areas where you can be in control, once you're ready to change your relationship.

As one of my business clients once put it:

"But I am looking for a guy who likes doing stuff, who wants to go out, who likes the outdoors and not sitting at home all day."

Then I bluntly put it to her, that if you seek that kind of guy then how do you expect him to find you, when you do exactly the opposite?

She was working from home, hardly ever getting out due to the internet nature of her business. Yes, similarities help. Or at least they help to start building or improving your relationships with others, as you have something in common to start from.

Relationships are not something you fix once into a stationary mood and then watch it to go stale, though the majority of people do approach their relationships in exactly this way.

It is ever-continuous moving process.

It's flowing, it's evolving.

It's progressing or it falls apart.

It is never solidified.

It is never permanent.

If it feels permanent – then the relationship more often than not - is stale.

For all the 'modern' or 'new age' thinkers, who believe in 'energy' and the reason I put the word energy in brackets is because the meanings are more varied than humans themselves.

While all the meditation and thinking processes as well as the Dalai Lama style are nice, it won't move your surroundings around you with the speed you need or want.

For those who are what we consider nowadays 'normal', ie, work nine to five (or seven to seven, as I was politely corrected by another friend of mine) you have a family to look after with hardly any allowances for luxuries such as a retreat at the meditation resort, and you're considered to be lucky if you manage to get just pure fun family holidays. You who consider new-age thinkers as those who 'lost it' – you are not far away from the truth.

It is more when you meet the aging 'new-age' thinker disappointed with the way progress is going that you should worry, for the rest of you, well - maybe consider one as your next conversationalist buddy.

Enough of the verbal abuse and teasing.

At the end of the day we all have several personalities which we use depending on the situation.

For example, you can't behave like a child when you are at the board meeting in your company, yet it would be completely appropriate to be childish playing with your kids, wouldn't it?

Hence I am not here to tell you how to unite yourself and make yourself just one and only human being. We all have different facets of our personalities. Be that hipster, be that a child, be that a parent, be that a CEO.

It is better if you keep all of your personalities evolved, explored and enhanced.

There is nothing worse than keeping your emotions and personalities repressed. PAY ATTENTION...do not re-direct these tethered down emotions towards other purposes, like holding grudges for example.

While grudge is mentioned earlier on and a bit later here, a little can be mentioned now to demonstrate the grudge in relationship side of things.

Grudges are so common among Asian cultures and many others as well as British males and females of certain religious beliefs.

Anything that people can't deal with in their relationships makes them feel diminished out of their narcissistic imagination more so than the reality.

They start holding grudges against the 'offender' who may or may not even realise their wrongdoings.

The grudge, while still eating away at them from the inside, manifests to the outside world. And is usually seen in such behaviour patterns as trying to avoid the 'offender', trying to hurt the 'offender' physically, emotionally or by any means possible including spreading various rumours.

And there is an art to how they do it. It is quite a mastery and normally starts by diminishing the 'offender' in others eyes. Then, should the etiquette allow, and once the bad image is established for the now official 'offender', they move on to their side of the story. Or leave it there, and share their own side of the story only when the opportunity is more beneficial.

It is almost as though they want to be victimized and as though their deep pleasure is derived from feeling that someone has offended them or is trying to make their life difficult.

I met two women who had completely mastered such skills, one is Japanese pretending to be an English aristocrat and the other one is a pedigree-free American, pretending to be Thai aristocracy thanks to a rather convenient marriage opportunity.

Both are practically living on sustaining at all costs the image they want to project. I never said narcissism is bad, I do however consider it an illness.

So badly so, they've perfected their skills to a grand state and anyone questioning their pedigree or abilities or social status as a joke or as a harmless remark are cut out at once, excluded, shut down. There is no way they'll allow you to feel equal, unless there is something they need from you. It is painful to watch.

They will not talk to anyone who is of their real background, or lower than what they now pretend to be. Yes, the class system still exists and in the minds of many. Sadly it is the most prominent in the minds of those who do not belong. The identity crisis as I call it.

It is another issue in our modern society. If we dig deeper it is connected with our pandemic of narcissism. It is long recognised, it is a mental health issue. Some of you may even exclaim, "But Olga, you wrote the book 'How to be Selfish!'"

Here it is: being selfish is about one's needs (apart from the other negative meaning, when it means not to care about anyone else which is also a mental health issue) yet narcissists are in love with the mirror image of themselves. The mirror image that is derived from what others will tell or 'show' them.

In reality it is very painful and extremely exhausting to sustain such an image and many narcissists are deeply depressed behind the closed door of their carefully orchestrated theatre performances.

The funny part is, that the smarter or shall I say more life-smart the person is and especially the more socially equipped, more often than not they are more open, friendly and humble. They have no need to compensate for their inequalities with psychologically-draining and harmful games.

We simply and bluntly can't pretend we are not social creatures and work so hard to isolate ourselves from the rest, either through fashion, beautiful material possessions, forming our tribes or a socially disconnected class structures. That is a very big part of who we are. If we do not exercise our basic need to socialise, the same as eating or drinking, we get ill. And it's contagious. Those who are around us get ill too. We are responsible for making ourselves ill and then contaminating others. Be that with our ill desires or sick and manipulative games.

And then of course there is this 'belonging' part. I happen to know an English gentlemen who has immigrated to Thailand from England in order to avoid the pretentiousness in England, only to return later with his Thai bride and be and embrace the same pretentiousness but now 'on his terms' for a wedding in London. Yes he made sure he brought her parents as well, to show his status and importance.

That is fine; play the game that feeds your needs. Belonging is an extremely 'painful' part and why wouldn't it be when you are born into …….. Feel free to put whatever is right in your case, but the presence of at least one more human is guaranteed. Should you be separated at one point or another from those you belong with – the sense of needing to belong can only increase.

I myself have been separated from my parents or those I loved dearly so often that at one point I had to educate myself not to crave belonging just to keep my sanity intact. Only years later I've discovered by chance that it works both ways. As you seek to belong the others seek to belong too.

As you seek, others are seeking.

It is so strong; you can literally manipulate or 'influence', as my clients prefer, others from the comfort of your chair.

But all the routes you can take to manipulate others into believing whatever you are trying to present of yourself in this world, do have its roots in our history, our upbringing and now our habits.

Habits. Forget about breaking them, that simply DOES NOT work.

There should be another book purely on how to create new habits and forget completely about removing the bad ones. So strong is their power, that only once you build a new habit that will be stronger enough than you're at least 20 years of age, you have a chance of substituting the transgressor.

I get it.

I hear that.

Now tell me how difficult it is to stop smoking if you are a regular smoker? That is if you do manage to stop at all, right?

Any habits I mean here, are just the same. Be that habits or social games.

Be that habits of social and cultural nature. Still echoing gender, stereotypical related issues anyone?

Did you know that women still earn on average less per hour then men on similar jobs? Worldwide.

Yes, still.

Did you know that it is only circa the 60s and 70s that the UK parliament passed laws giving women the right to equal pay? Did you know that women could not even vote till

1918? That is in Britain. I do not know the statistics from other countries but surely it must be similar.

According to my experience, it only get's worse.

Did you know that despite the existing laws in the UK, women still do not always have the same access to promotion and better-paid jobs as men do? Did you know that no man can give a birth, as yet?

I am not protecting women here, yet it sounds rather unreasonable to have double standards from both sides, men and women. Habits are difficult to change. Think quitting smoking and then correlate it to the cultural habits.

There you may possibly need to control only yourself to change the smoking habit. And what about when we speak about implementing new social habits? Such as equality rights etc?

In a few countries women are still second tier compared to men.

And getting back to civilized countries, women are still not respected and their opinion cannot possibly be considered by aging executives who were born during the time that women stayed at home and husbands were the providers. Habits!

They, the aging executives, only complain when they need to divorce their wives and suddenly expect them to be complete independent women.

Women on the other hand insist their male should be a provider while women should be concentrating mainly... on themselves. We are all confused.

The first changes came suddenly and are still not happening equally across the world.

Don't forget that above statistics are only for the UK and in many countries men still have the upper hand. On the other hand in countries like Brazil it is not so much that men have the upper hand but the over population of women compared to men is what causes a bizarre effect.

Based on the rule of 'supply and demand' currently men in Brazil do have an upper hand. They even have a saying 'the first wife'. They even have a state where they have about 21 women per one man.

A rather funny effect of the power struggle can be observed in Italy where men still live with their mums till about age of 40 and it considered to be normal. Italian men are so repressed by their mums that they compensate their urges of dominance with their explicitly exploited nature of their television programs. Women can only appear on TV when they're wearing next to nothing, or presented as lower beings next to men. One recent popular evening quiz show has a young, scantily dressed woman climb into a plexi-glass cage each episode, where she remains throughout, responding to the jokey put-downs from the host with obsequious smiles.

Do not forget that many women of these generations are still alive and influencing their daughters and their granddaughters. It is not so much the Hollywood movies that are lately blamed for an increased desire for happy-ever-marriage but family pressure, including fathers and grandfathers.

Most of the well-off and independent women came to work with me to address the pressure they where experiencing from their families and peers on the subject of marriage and family. They really were confused.

It wasn't the fact that they were in need or desired to get married, they were leading very happy lives and they usually had a long-term partner or occasional flings and had no desire to settle down unless the union would be great for both parties. Some plainly didn't see the point in marriage.

I even remember the one emergency session I had with one of my politician clients, when the whole session was taken up by her monologue regarding a guy who isn't what she wants, but his and her family pressure to get married was crushing her confidence and she almost agreed to marry. Thanks to that session she was prevented from going into the wrong marriage. No, I did not tell her why he is wrong, I've simply asked her to tell me what she knows about him and his history of relationships. Paradoxically the guy was married before, and he has been in several long-term relationships. However after a while, once he'd managed to manipulate them into his 'perfect woman' he was bored of his next toy and he'd seek a new 'challenge' shall we say, where my client happened to 'fit' the profile.

When we are under pressure we close our eyes to what we do not want to see and concentrate on what will help us to relive the pressure or pain.

We are too weak to deal with the pressure of others who act out of their own fear and prejudice. If as much time was spent on building healthy social relationships based on a mutual respect and at least an understanding or an agreement to SEE the other person's point of view, as on watching the TV, reading the news and searching the internet, we'd be better off already with all our mental health issues. We'd at the very least pursue the desires that come from our heart, rather than from unrealistic media set expectations for pure commercial reasons. And it works! While the media succeeds at selling us high expectations, we fail to pause and acknowledge what our own expectations are.

During one of the events I've attended, Tamsin Greig was speaking about the charity she supports, The Tearfund. In particular she spoke regarding a program concentrating on the welfare of women. According to the charity, 70 percent of those living in poverty are women, and more than half a million women die in pregnancy and childbirth each year. However it is gender-based violence that causes more deaths and disability. Mainly among women aged 15 to 44.

Women are still as vulnerable as before. According to the American Journal of Public Heath, 48 women each hour are raped in the Democratic Republic of Congo.

While for some that seems to be 'normal' considering they have what they call the Second Congo War, how about us? We still have rape issues.

Two of my closest friends, independently, got gang raped. At a time, there was not much on offer to heal their psychological and physical traumas. One girl has found strength and family support to take the case to the court. Mainly because two girls were involved. Both 14 at a time.

The attackers didn't even care my friend had her dog with her, they grabbed all three of them from the street into their van. While continuously raping them passing via their circle they'd continuously cut them using the variety of knives they had on them accompanying each cut with threats of death. My friend credited the fact that due to one guy only, who has freaked out it has gone too far, they somehow managed to abandon them somewhere in a forest. Though her friend insist it's because they thought they did kill them, as they were senseless by the time they were through with them.

Since the attackers were soldiers and the area relatively small it didn't take long to find the offenders and prosecute them. Needless to say since I was the first to help my friend out psychologically, once her life got restored she wanted to do nothing with me for I was a reminder of her pain.

The other girl wasn't as lucky, 16 at the time, being gang raped she couldn't take the case to the court and she even hid it from her family. It is pure coincidence she has even survived. I still have a haunting image of her description implanted in my head, of her drenched in her own blood crawling to the nearest house. After sharing her story with me and slowly getting on with her life, she eventually did share the events with her seriously ill mother. The last time I saw her she was in relationship with a new guy who seemed to be very caring and protective of her. It was painful to see, once a tomboy like girl who was stronger than me in fights, completely crushed and with the scared animal-like look permanently residing in her eyes now. That was the very girl who taught me tricks how to deal with hooligans and helped to get 'respect' from the teens of my own age when I was teaching them. It was this girl who has helped me to establish my boundaries with a boy who was particularly sexually aggressive towards me in my school. She was my strength. She was that bad girl who I needed as my friend to get through life as a 'good' girl. After I relocated to London – I never saw her again.

The other example that actually did get a lot of publicity is the gang rape of 23-year-old woman in India, who suffered massive internal injuries and died nearly two weeks later.

You know why there is no conclusion to the book? Because the issues and illnesses we possess belong to all of us. No matter what culture, country, sex or else we belong to. Rapes are regular events everywhere. The circumstances and the public reaction is different. But the abuse from those who are mentally ill – is the same. Everywhere.

Remembering the reaction of my friend who got raped just years prior the other friend of mine, I suspect it's for the best that we no longer know each other whereabouts. There is no need to remind my friend of her past pain. I am referring to a country that was not at WAR. I am referring to a country which is a European country and not even India where women's rights are still near non-existent. I doubt any of other countries are that dissimilar. We just do not speak about it much. And yes, women aren't the only victims here.

I just wanted to make the point. Maybe, just maybe, if we'd work on regarding our illnesses as power struggles and physical anomalies as to raping those who are weaker or smaller or both, be that men or women, boys or girls. Possibly by advocating equality a little bit harder by explaining the priorities of each sex, just maybe we'd succeed in reducing the harm many ill people cause to others. There should be more education about the importance of another human life. Forget the sexual gender. Children really need to be educated about the value of a human, any human life first.

Many of our secluded behaviours come nowadays from a lack of respect for another human life, which is not even ours to take. What's wrong with our own lives? Why do we have such urges to leave and control others, just because we fail to control and to understand ourselves?

How can anyone in a healthy state of mind even vaguely believe he or she can control others when failing to control his or her own life? You are bonkers if you truly believe that you are socially well equipped yet you have no control over your own life and your own circumstances. It is a pure fear that drives you to such lengths to control others. It's almost like 'kill them, before they kill you'. Your fear is what's killing you or at the very least eating you from inside. And the fear is not even real. You've created your own prison out of all the fears you've borrowed from others.

Schools are in a hurry to educate children's sexuality while forgetting the fact the gender differences is not something that they need to absorb first. We have this weird need to belong and to be better at the same time. By providing differences in gender we provide the starting point of separation. Such creations as one-sex schools and public in particular are now creating a growing army... no, not gay. The growing army of misogynists.

And on personal relationships.

Men complain about women, women blame men and vice versa.

But is it really that it is someone's fault? We are so used to the instant gratification in these modern days, we forget it takes time to build relationships. We have become so materialised that our mind is infected with the perception that other human beings are possibly like toys or worse, should always read our mind and agree with us 100 percent.

Why?

I mean what did you do to ensure that the other person will agree with you? And what's in it for you?

I constantly meet successful men and women who are in a relationship and are unhappy.

How do they deal with that?

Both parties shut their eyes and get on as they can and possibly even with a romance on the side. Instant gratification.

It is easier to break and buy a new thing than to restore the old one and besides how often do you really succeed at restoring the old thing to the 'new' glory just as it used to be?

Relationships aren't a material thing. They are spiritual.

You can't simply glue it together once it's damaged, there is work and investment time required of you.

Relationships aren't easy, but then life isn't. Relationships are there to enrich your experiences via sharing information, moments of life, feelings, emotions, physical moments and more and more. Building, rebuilding, participating in relationships with others is a part of our life experience.

The fact that you find a new lover who appreciates you more than your other half at home, does not mean it will last forever, because let me tell you something. If you are rubbish at one relationship – you will be rubbish at another relationship. Until you learn....

Yes there are wrong marriages, arranged, forced, through some sort of agreement for financial, political, PR or other reasons. And yes some people do grow apart. Under no circumstances am I suggesting you should stay in a wrong relationship no matter what. I suggest that there may be a chance that the problem in relationship is you. You simply start taking your partner for granted. You simply expect more.

The most fascinating aspect I find when one of the partners is trying to amend the situation and tries little steps such as buying flowers, arranging holidays and then the other partner will go for an attack with accusations like "Why? What do you want now?", "Are you seeing someone?", "Why would you do that, who cares now?" and possibly even more painful and hurtful phrases than I've mentioned here.

The Greek Tragedy here is that both parties are not communicating.

One woman complained to me "But the minute I say something about feelings he shuts himself down and finds excuses to leave." Yes, that is still common, and not just among men. Silent treatment anyone?

Yet if you both care about each other and you are willing to try then you do need to talk about the big elephant in the room. And you need to talk in a way that your partner understands. It is an effort. But from what I've been told, Rome hasn't been built in a day. Nor any relationship.

It is true that my first husband has proposed to me on the third day after he met me and only few months later we got married (we'd have got married there and then but the registrar was fully booked). Yet our relationship did not start to fully blossom till about four years into our marriage. We weren't sure about many things and we weren't even sure we wanted to be married in fact. We just gave it a go. He didn't want to lose me and I thought, there is a man who understands that I have my needs and desires and ambitions to fulfill. We fought, we made love, we argued, we kissed, we smiled, we laughed, we hated each other, we loved each other, we blamed each other, we worshiped each other.

The relationship was so contagious that it didn't take long for all my friends around me to get involved in relationships as well. In fact any great relationship will inspire even heartless bachelor to get married or at the very least to find a partner to live with. Because the joy of sharing your experience with someone you genuinely respect and care about – multiples.

Everyone wants to be happy and everyone dreams about that understanding half, or a friend, or a partner, or… but definitely someone special in their lives. I'll treasure for ever that day in my life when approximately four years through our marriage I looked at Lambros (my first husband's name) and said that I felt as though I met him only yesterday, that's how happy he was making me feel. He turned around, came close, hugged me and said "I only now know what love is. I know it sounds strange, but I now love you even more than the day we got married."

And for a few years we absolutely had a dream marriage. I knew that was not common, and in the relationship I was the one 'shutting down', but he cared, he took his time and he was there for me, and most importantly – he was there WITH me.

And if you think that relationship issues are the only problem there is another aspect, it is considered to be as a stamp of social approval that you have to go out with someone. Even these days.

It is simply enough to ask someone in a large company whether they are as single as the rest and you can see them all boiling up and nearly screaming their head off to ensure they are NOT single. Happy or not happy – the motivation here is pure social status – the stamp of social approval that is. If I may ask here, so who's life do you live? Yours? Or of the image you've projected?

The difference is bigger than you can possibly imagine.

For starters…

Besides the fact that it is only about a century since in many countries women have the right to divorce their husbands and have equal rights, though not in all countries. We have a situation where women, in those countries where the rights are equal, at least on the paper or by law, the majority are brought up by their mothers, grandmothers or great grandmothers who are heavily influenced with the old mentality.

The changes were so fast and sudden and still far from being realised, women are almost locked in a frozen state.

The subconscious heavily dominates when it comes to the security of their offspring, ie marriage, a husband who is able (financially or physically is a different dialogue here altogether), while consciously women are understanding the need and advantage for independence. Women are trapped between the old classic and nouveau lifestyle. While men are completely tormented - 'so do you want the old style where we provide and own you or a new style where we are equal in which case we demand real equality'.

Add to that the 70 year old CEOs who are completely bedazzled with the fact they have to receive instruction from a young female consultant? What? Yes we still have age discrimination as well!

And so while we are all upside down and struggling with all the stresses of life and the new pressures of equality, add to it ever-changing sexual preferences.

That would really sort itself out if not for the biological instinct to reproduce and the biological need to spread. Naturlich, I am referring to women and men accordingly.

And what about children? So whose responsibility is it going to be now? Do you really expect the female to carry all the burden? Or a male in case the women are clearly taking advantage of their partners, as in the case of one very famous woman. We should keep her name out of here, although, in a way it is so common that it is kind of irrelevant. She is now 38 years old, got her degree, had a desire to get married and to have children as her co-adjusted Big Ben has demanded. She did that. Got a husband, got her child, got a journalist career. Then she thought "What now?" As you are well aware many are still neurotic when it comes to the next stage after "Happy Ever After".

She thought hang on, I can have a business as the next fun venture, so she goes on to create one, she gets her husband to join on board as the business progresses. The business takes off and she starts socialising a lot, a few more years down the line, the husband now runs their business from home so that he can look after the child. He is becoming boring to her and less adventurous next to all those hyper-excited, socially lubricated socialites of the male sex especially, then she starts looking at her husband through the adverse spectrum.

The next thing she does, she creates an adventurous liaison with the first available handsome man, who is also possibly in need of climbing the social ladder.

While I've used an example of a woman, the same applies for men. The phrase 'jump the counter' exists for a reason and so does the acceptance of the most acceptable and respectable form of male prostitution (females aren't really rejected here).

And the shopping for 'the next best', most satisfying companion begins, just like in a supermarket. Sometimes you'll have to go for a past-due date and some times you can afford a tender Wagyu Steak. Really depends on your abilities to supply. Where supply can mean: almighty dollar/pound or the currency of your choice, social network with a generous opportunity to jump ahead on career ladder, sexual availability, or other possibilities to satisfy the needs, desires, cravings, aches, perversions or in some cases even deep (as deep as your cavities allow you) spiritual experiences.

We no longer want to work on our social or communication skills because we heavily rely on some sort of physical presence, exchange or satisfaction.

Why work on our relationships where we are bored when we can work a bit harder on earning more or losing extra weight or colouring those dark roots or bleaching our anuses and getting a better toy for our next period or brief encounter with another human being. What's wrong with us? Did we somehow jump the line of being satisfied and can't stop our habit of hoarding and hoarding? It was hoarding provisions and basic needs earlier in our humanity or at least we choose to think so, and now it is hoarding in anything vaguely material and human.

Our hoarding skills now differ only from our need to prove our social status. To ourselves that is.

Because NO ONE EVER CARES ABOUT YOU REALLY.

It is always about THEM.

Get it?

PART 2

The character traits we posses,
we fail to treat as mental health illnesses.

5

Living the DREAM....
or a delusional self-perception

At times it really does feel extraordinary watching and listening to advertisers trying to capture our attention with magic words 'Live the Dream', 'Imagine…'.

How far away are we really from living the dream? We do dream often, if not in our daydreams then at least at night. You've possibly had at least one dream when on wakening you've questioned whether it was a dream in fact or a memory of reality?

Let me draw your attention to perceptions. The perception we have of ourselves and the way we believe what and who we are. Each of us has an inner image of ourselves; how we perceive ourselves for better or for worse.

We need to remind ourselves that our own image of ourselves is somewhat 'imaginary'.

How do you know who you are? You compare yourself to those around you. Should you be born in isolation on a secluded island, you would believe that the world and you are one of a kind.

When trying to explain to my clients I state: you are not poor, your lifestyle is too expensive. What do I mean by this?

So you are working in Britain on a basic managerial level with an annual salary of approximately 70k, you have a mortgage and a lifestyle to support. Perhaps even a family to feed as well. You decide to spend an evening with your company CEOs, some of which need not work, they are that wealthy and you draw a comparison. You feel somewhat poor next to them. If your partner is accompanying you along, you may be nagged later on how well your boss has done in life.

You feel even more unsatisfactory. The rat race is on. However that the very wealthy person in fact may have received a large inheritance. It is also possible that the very wealthy person in fact has lots of debts and he can't sleep at night. Whether wealthy or not, his or hers (whoever seems to be wealthier) life – is not YOURS.

You feel somewhat poor and not senior or successful enough by the benchmarks you create, your self-esteem is not of the highest level. You put yourself under constant pressure because you know there is still a great deal of work for you to complete before you can reach the partnership or the CEO's level, or higher. I have no clue which pressures you have subjected yourself to. For all I know you could be an academic working in a science department beating yourself up as your colleague just won a Nobel prize in the literary department. You know you'll never achieve the same since your chosen area of talent is in mathematics.

On the other hand, should you collapse emotionally and physically, choosing to quit your job, sell your property and move to another country with a less expensive lifestyle such as India for example. Your perception of yourself will change in a blink of an eye you'll see yourself as wealthy. Here, compared to others – you are rich. Here compared to others, it is you now who can afford not to work for a while. It is you now who will get the position of CEO thanks to your some-what privileged background or work-experience. It is you whose wealth is acknowledged by others who aspire to be in your shoes. It is you who can afford to live the dream!

It is as simple and as basic as, if you are weak enough to sustain the self-image you crave, change the surroundings and people. As I often say to my clients, any of your goals can be compared to your first dream-partner image. If you are a 14 year old babe your ideal boyfriend most probably is some kind of rock star idol. If you are a 30+ successful career woman the ideal boyfriend would be a CEO or a guy who owns his own successful company.

It's slightly different with guys. If you are desperate, you drink beer and any girl is beautiful or you drink more heavy stuff and pass out. Once you are more successful, you'll hunt down the girl who is more of a trophy type, as she is a part of your new image. Yes, this maybe over simplified and general. These examples are only given to you to explain how if you change your surroundings and people around you once you change your inner image of yourself. That's an easy path.

Here we are more interested in an alternative pattern, chang-ing your inner image first in order to have the relationship you seek, be that with work colleagues, your family or your dear beloved one, or with the new world opening up – any other being! You've no need to up and move across the world, the change starts closer to home - within.

If you've ever ridden horses, you'll understand what I mean.

First you have to break your own mental hurdles. A handsome horse is supposed to respect and submit to you. When I took horse-riding lessons, I could never understand how this tall and gorgeous horse would ever listen to me. And it didn't – til my trainer change my mind pattern. It's the same here, every day, with any being around you. You do not do it with physical power, you do it with your mind, which you are to train for your own benefit. Many country leaders know it is not armour, but ideas that are the most damaging to their power.

Pussy Riot anyone?

A little step sideways. Many people often have an inner image of themselves damaged by emotional scars, it is almost as if you possess some sort of recording mechanism in you for anything and everything ever said about you and to you, which forms your inner opinion of yourself on your behalf. Sadly that is not correct, for it was influenced by what others told you and people firstly refer to themselves whenever they comment on you. Ever heard a parent saying to a child: you are a failure! Only out of their own frustration and being afraid that their children will end up just like them: a failure? They are scared. And possibly you act out of fear. Even your efforts with your highly paid job are driven by **FEAR**.

And you know what? The joke is on them!

Your inner opinion is hardly true and is hardly valid, because what other people told you about you – is more about them. And you do not know your own opinion of yourself and that is the beauty, at least in general terms! The opinions you stored so far, 85 percent belong to others. The inner opinion of yourself you have so far sets the limits of what you can and cannot accomplish. All your boundaries and perimeters are based on OTHER people's experiences.

That is quite *ill*, don't you think?

Think about it. Your entire life, you form an opinion of yourself not based on the actuality. It is like you are on some sort of hallucinogenic drug. Your image of yourself is a wild imagination you borrow from those around you. I mean, how often do you hear "He gave me my confidence back" or "she made me realise that I can do it" or "she made me feel a man again!"?

If you still are trying to argue with me on that point. Let me give you a different model. How many parents are telling their children: "Don't talk to the strangers"?

How many individuals who listened to these words of caution during their childhood later face issues when talking to a complete stranger. Depending on that reaction you may or may not close your new business deal, secure a date with a gorgeous woman, handsome man or simply fail to benefit from meeting a new great friend? The amount of people who find themselves shell-shocked at the idea of attending a networking event they have never been to before by themselves is as large as the turnover of hamburgers sold by McDonalds each day.... worldwide.

Here, I'd like to add - unusual as it may sound to you, or perhaps it may make you feel uncomfortable: respect towards yourself is the best way to create power. It has nothing to do with Narcissism. Narcissism is the latest disease of our society.

Narcissism is not so much about self-love as some people might think. To remind yourself the pure meaning you simply wish to visit Galleria Nazionale d'Arte Antica in Rome and absorb the *Narcissus* painting by Caravaggio, where the figure of Narcissus is locked in a circle with his reflection, surrounded by darkness, so that the only reality is inside this self-regarding loop. The gospel of narcissism is unhealthy due to a disturbance in the sense of self. The reflection. Not you, yourself. Narcissism is about love of an image. An image of what is projected. An image others project onto you and you accept without hesitation.

Voila. We have just diagnosed you with narcissism. Because if you think carefully of the actions you take to sustain the image and the social status of yourself, it is what is projected onto you. It is your very Narcissism that controls your decision to buy this particular car. It is your very Narcissism that makes a young girl shop in Primark and save enough to purchase the Mulberry bag. It is your very Narcissism that drives you up the career ladder at times. It is Narcissism that helps your dear beloved author to sustain her maddening shopping habits, for she falls in love with the image of herself wearing that new dress. Just like that. Just like you.

6

Violence

Violence is the tricky one. In a nutshell, on one side violence grows out of fear. Fear that whatever you believe in or whatever you think is right or good can be perceived by others as incorrect and not fact at all. More bitter than that is the fear you can be persuaded that someone else's ideas and beliefs are right and your thoughts are wrong.

The other aspect of violence is born out of fear of death.

While varying in-depth research has been done to prove we are more than just our physical body, fear of death is still at the base of all fears. Just consider for a while you know you cannot die; on one hand it may give an impression that our fears may reduce; in reality the knowledge of an afterlife or even immortality would result in most of us fearing and worrying more, which could spark outbursts of violence even further.

It would no longer be, I 'go' and after me I don't care. Be that as it may, the majority still believe in death. And it may as well to say "I kill you first, before you kill me."

As Oscar Wilde once said "I'm not young enough to know everything" which leads us to the other fear leading to violence.

"The more I learn, the more I learn how little I know." - Socrates

Take the old example of tomatoes. When not so long ago Americans and English thought tomatoes where poisonous while Italians were snacking away on delicious tomato-dishes. At first the breakthrough came thanks to a decision that tomatoes where unfit for eating, rather than poisonous. Later however due to intensive consumption by Italians and Spanish, tomatoes where given another chance.

Russians still tell horror tales of famous poisonous potatoes when Peter the Great had introduced them first by mistake, most where eating the potato-fruits which where poisonous instead of the large main potato.

Ignorance is no longer affordable and in a way it is the responsibility of those who know to share.

The whole worldly society is a mere representation of blind people examining the different parts of an elephant and arguing who is right, when one part is examining the head, the other part is checking out the leg and third party is clearly stuck with the tail.

The missing point is in a complete misunderstanding of our life as it is and the universe around us. The lack of understanding ourselves only adds to the all-encompassing confinement called 'self-delusion'.

Should a human being lead a stagnant lifestyle, in the language of biology stagnant means dead. The more motionless the lifestyle you are subjected to, the less you are evolving, the less you are evolving the faster you are degrading. With the degradation process fears flow in plenty. The more we are scared the more we feel the need to protect ourselves.

And why not you? We are programmed to follow examples. The best examples we follow are our own very governments. The United States is afraid the oil controlling power will be taken by someone else. Russia is afraid of anyone who will claim to possess the strongest nuclear reactors.

England?

China?

Japan, who have simply lost the plot and possibly will take time to interconnect again with the rest of the world?

Africa? Africa is the country that reminds me of a child who receives help physically, yet denies the presence of help in their minds.

And simply name any other country. Each government is afraid of something.

We follow dutifully.

The fact is many new discoveries including developments in mind, mind theory and the existence of the etheric body are kept well behind closed doors. Any findings regarding other life forms outside of our planet earth are kept under lock and key. Partially our leaders are afraid, partially we all are afraid. It is as though we have another disease – we are afflicted with fear.

If our leaders were not afraid, there would be only one centralised structure.

One country. One government.

All the discoveries and scientific progress would belong to most of us.

That thought alone would send most of us into shivers.

Just think about it. Our upbringing has pumped up our ego and has trained us to think we are meant to be the best and the strongest, we are meant to have the best or we have to be of the better class. And I am definitely one to talk, it has taken me a whole decade and the transformation isn't even close to completion, to understand the self-delusion we live in.

Violence doesn't end just there. It goes in the following chain structure:

Fear of death leads to -

Fear of others in power leads to –

Feeling the need to prove that leads to –

Bulling that leads to –

Verbal or psychological abuse that leads to

The need to have more of everything, be that sex, be that material possessions, that leads to –

I want to have the best, the biggest etc etc, that leads to –

The self delusional belief that I'm the best, I'm the strongest, I'm in control…..And of course you are until the next best, stronger, in greater control individual comes knocking at your door.

People in fear feel isolated and the more isolated they feel, they believe help is nowhere to be found. When in fact the help is available they are just unable to see it at that moment. We are all in the same boat, more isolated and fearing. No one is out to get us, we are so overwhelmed by our illness that our sight and senses become impaired.

Our daily routine has now become more technologically advanced but has left our emotions and senses disadvantaged. More detached. Think of the amount of times we have considered texting 'no' without looking the person in the eye, reducing our embarrassment and discomfort. Avoiding all psychological feelings which would normally accompany such dealings.

It is simply an acute kind of self-delusion. It starts with thinking along the following lines: that the boss hates you or that your colleagues are not respecting you, or that nationals of your country of residence are against your kind. The longer you consider this, the more paranoid you become, the wider the spread.

The next thing you see is your partner is against you, should you keep your thoughts playing, you are not far away from believing the whole world is against you.

Really?

Let me surprise you.

NO ONE READS YOUR MIND. Well most people can't read your mind. They simply get on with their life confused to why you are so aggressive or unhappy lately. Why is it that you are such a bully, neurotic, psychopath or plain violent.

People like that are ill. Countries like that are ill. Governments are ill.

They need love and understanding.

It is not going to be easy, yet one side has to start first.

While many readers support charity and already doing greater good for the humanity, you forget those who are the closest. If your close ones are violent, think of the child who lacks ability to express him or her self, and grows so frustrated, starts using violence. People like that need help. Children like that need help. They do not need an argument, they do not need an explanation but simple refusal to play along will help at the beginning. It really is like fire, you need to keep adding wood to keep it going. Should you be involved with someone like that, distance yourself as much as you can and let the person come around. Some don't, for they are so deep in themselves. At this stage no one can or should help them for they need to understand it is up to them.

After years and years of working with my clients, I realise how blind we are to our own stamina, power and ability to produce and create. We believe we are weak and not enough. We believe we have to and should. It takes me a few sessions to bring their strength back. I am not referring to 'I can do anything'. Not at all. Quite the opposite.

We can't do anything and we are not able to achieve anything we want unless we work on ourselves first, which in turn requires a lot of mental discipline. Considering the majority of people can't even keep up with regularly attending their gym or controlling their eating habits, the popular so called 'coaches' of today telling us "I can make you anything you want!" are spinning a line of BULLSHIT. We are not even close to achieving anything we want until we learn about ourselves.

These so called 'coaches' are hardly able to sustain their own mental discipline. There are exceptions and don't forget you don't need a great teacher, quite the opposite, you only need the one teacher who can take you to the next few levels, hence there is food for everyone ;).

Once you authentically respect yourself, you plainly can't humiliate others. Any form of violence including toward oneself or more commonly labeled 'bulling' is the result of feeling fear, but the subconscious feeling of fear.

Fear is caused by experiencing too many complexes or anxieties at any given moment. Fear is against progress or any type of evolution, as I prefer to call it when explaining to clients. Such words are not accepted easily by those who struggle emotionally or financially and definitely not for the weak-minded. If you do not care about yourself, if you do not love yourself: deep inside you feel unworthy of success. You fail to understand you can control not just your thoughts and your beliefs but also the direction of your attitude. Such thoughts and attitude may materialise in every day health issues, negative events or unexpected complications. Complications at work and complications in your personal life.

It is not by chance that I bring the subject of self-respect and self-love here. For years I've been telling my clients, if you do not respect yourself – how do I know that I can respect you? It really is difficult and requires far more effort and time to achieve any desired outcome without support, respect and love from within. Plain and simply: without true, unconditional and tender love for yourself you are not adding to anyone's life.

Worse of all, you are robbing yourself, by yourself.

7

Yet Another Groundhog Day

On the day I successfully passed the sailing theory exam, my classmates and I went for a drink in a City Bar. The day was relatively nice and not as chilly as usual. We gradually dispersed into smaller groups to converse.

I ended up chatting with a lovely guy who at the time was restoring his recently acquired industrial barge.

Neither classmates nor the guy I conversed with knew my background nor the events which had just occurred in my life. Rather conveniently for the purpose of this book I have realised how much we assume rather than checking the background story. And as I was sharing my dreams of sailing around Greek islands and taking holidays in the Hamptons, the guy suddenly took a different turn, stopped and directly accused me of being ignorant of real life. When I asked him to explain his accusations, he simply suggested I follow his example. As he had pointed out, as a good person – he is planning to take his children to India to show them that there is so much poverty in the world and that they should appreciate what they have. Needless to say, the conversation came to a full stop when I said – "I've lived through poverty, I had enough. It is for some time now, I've chosen a different life and under no circumstances would I want to be part of poverty again."

Funny that, when you've experienced it, you have a completely different understanding to those so-called spoiled people, and those brought up wealthy or with decent standards. I still find it highly amusing when so many of the people who are brought up in complete financial security, visit some poor areas and suddenly come up with saviour ideas, blindly unaware of the underlying circumstances and the culture and motives behind. Just like doctors keep treating the side effects rather than causes. It's time we accept that if we haven't lived the same life we cannot be truly aware of the causes.

As one of my friends has politely pointed out, wouldn't it be nice if some people enjoyed better conditions? She is of course correct, but by just giving away things without any additional emotional support and education, it is really of very little help. We are humans and it's not that simple. We cannot pop a pill and everything is sorted. As with the latest cancer treatments, there's a consultation, there are sessions with psychologists and there's the treatment.

We need to approach the subject with a more complex and insightful strategy.

Let's stop treating just the symptoms and stop causing even more undesired side effects.

I shall share with you some of my experiences to demonstrate this point of view.

It is almost like an amazing conversation with a French computer scientist I had just on the day of French elections in 2012. He stated that he wants communism in his country and I hurriedly blasted out my opinion:

"I've lived through the communism. It does not work. What more proof do you want?"

While we had a heated debate as a result of my remark and due to the strength of each of our beliefs as well as a respect for each other we decide not to escalate the argument to a grandeur level; we did switch to discussing fluffy kittens at a later point.

It was the next morning during the language conference in Washington that he stated: "If this person actually has experienced communism and I haven't, it may be that she has a valid point."

I am not merely saying I am right. Because frankly I do not know what's best for YOU. Unless I meet you and YOU tell me what's best for you. I am saying don't just blindly follow what others preach to you. They are blind too. We all are blind, for the future is unknown. Not till we learn to direct it, direct ourselves that is.

Think. And think for yourself.

Don't just blindly think it's great because the idea sounds amazing.

Don't just assume the person in front of you is smart, because one has three Masters degrees.

Don't think that the person in front of you is right because he happens to be male, a philosopher with an English pedigree.

I've met someone who, according to their career position and their three Masters degrees, has respect and is thought to be a very intelligent woman. Well, then she opened her mouth and made an idiotic remark about a real life situation when she was stopped for speeding in the United States:

"I really did not understand why is it that I gave an American policeman a bribe and he did not take it and got offended."

I honestly wanted to do nothing with her. It was a great eye opener for me – academic degrees do not mean you are smart. They just mean just that – a degree. Being life smart and being book smart are far from each other, possibly farther that the moon and sun are from the earth.

It is time to break our institutionalised values and review them. It is time to keep only what is working, or at least we suspect or strongly believe is working and substitute or adjust the rest.

The world has never before been evolving at the speed it does now. It is time we adjust to these changes and embrace them, and help each other with the missing knowledge as well as with an understanding.

It is time to take responsibility into our hands. Each and every one of us is now responsible. The sooner we get it, the sooner the rest will follow, the sooner there will be an opportunity and the right HOPE. The sooner we reduce the epidemic of Mental Health illnesses, the better.

So, regarding the conversation with the guy highlighting my 'ignorance' and telling me I need to travel to India. Believe it or not, as often in my case with all my mind blowing simultaneousness and pure luck, I went to India just a month after we've had our conversation.

It was a chance and I took it.

Sadly for the guy, I did not see what he saw.

He saw India as a poor country. I saw it as a community who refuses to move on from pre-westernised methods of living.

The class system is so strongly in their blood that I doubt anyone truly challenges it. The few that do, do so by moving abroad and not in their own country. And why would they? It is convenient to keep the class system in order, sorry, it is convenient to keep the karma tradition because it allows you to make sure that people do as they are told. It supports their class system. Because it is all driven into every little newborn heart through fear.

But if you think that all classes are naive, you are far from the truth. It is at times convenient to simply complain rather than do anything about it, because that will require you to take responsibility and possibly pain, which is far stronger than the desire. But let's leave the poor people of India, or China, or Russia… let's get back to the modern civilization, or so it is called nowadays, such countries as the USA and Great Britain.

Naturally, when we live for too long in one location, especially if we are born there, we do not notice many things as shocking or wrong since they come as a given.

It is only when we travel that we do notice something horrifying or out of place and only then and IF we start analysing do we realise we actually live next to the very same situation every day back at our own homes, on our own streets.

While seemingly the inequality gap has disappeared after slavery abolishment, the gap is even wider - if anything in a multidimensional way, because our own struggle in order to satisfy our ego has created a new way to disengage ourselves from others. We usually nickname it *identity*.

And so we leave, completely caught up in that self-delusional and self-indulging structure of the identity we pick or the identity we are given.

And then of course there is a situation when we either fight to support the identity or… we fight to break free of the existing identity and create the one we want to have or the one we aspire to.

Often both and at the same time. Often blindly. For to live a chosen identity is another sophisticated and quite an exhausting game. Just like Narcissism.

And so many of our ancestors have traveled many miles to reach the better future, the better identity.

The United States.

A great country.

The land of opportunities… or is it?

One sunny day, I was on my way to the United States Botanic Garden in Washington DC. I do prefer to use the local transportation rather than a taxi for it always makes me feel uncomfortable and lets me immerse into the real city life.

I took the metro.

I started from the University station and the majority of few passengers were students, universities workers and academics. As we passed by other stations the carriages filled with a variety of human forms, the majority representing characters from *The Wire*, music rap video clips, some dressed like pimps, others like whores, most of them seemed to be on drugs of some sort. It was outside rush hour, a time when everyone has the privilege of the metro transportation in the comfort of their own seat.

There was a couple seated in front of me. The couple consisted of one white shapeless large woman with a disabled hand (yet she was able to hold her beer can with the 'disadvantaged' hand) and a more sober looking, equally overweight yet somehow shapelier black woman. Both seemed to be in their forties though time had not been kind to them and their lack of personal hygiene reflected their hard times. While their state was more or less equal in their dress code and state of mind, the white woman seem to be at an extreme stage of that state. She wore hotpants. Her low cut top was so low that the bra which failed to cover and to hold what's left of her breasts was revealed. The skin resembled that of Morels. Her eyes rolled up to the top of her lids.

On my left there was a young couple with a guy dressed as a rapper with all the appropriate symbolism attached, looking spaced out and unconcerned when his seemingly equally spaced out girlfriend spotted an advert for a free burger in the newspaper, read by a guy opposite them. The minute he put the paper down she, satisfied with her observational skills, grabbed the paper at once and tore the ad. For free food. She then proudly paraded the piece of newly acquired treasure in front of her half senseless rap-boyfriend.

There were more... more varied people. Who unlike their comrades in poor countries have access to all the wealth and basics they need.

It is a new breed.

A breed that spreading cancerously contaminating everyone and everywhere, who like them, have access to everything and anything should they choose to make an effort for it.

What's happening?

We fail to recognise fear. Fear of being in need. Sadly we only consider our physical needs as our instant priority.

When you are poor or in need, you desperately try to make ends meet. Once the needs are met, many get confused and splurge whatever they have as soon as they can. Hence my saying providing the food for the needy ones is not a solution but a temporarily help. The same applies to help with any other basic needs. As my agent, who has a different opinion of charities to mine, has stated that even he agrees that there is a time to give and there is a time to educate.

He wasn't referring to the schooling education as such he was referring to sharing knowledge and educating with skills. Knowledge and skills that can stay for life with those in need.

What happens next is the most astonishing enigma. While poor countries struggle to fight the poverty and famine. The citizens of richer countries struggle to find what to do with their time?! They'll work all right, should they fail to put themselves on benefits or earn supplies by other means. They'll lead the usual clichéd life. Some will even form families and then their lives will revolve around sustaining those families, usually children though in some cases that would be looking after their elderly parents.

What has happened with the hunger for life itself?

Where is the zest, which seems to creep in only at the times when you are ready to go to the other side?

Why such apathy?

Still, let's stick to poor versus rich. It's easier. That's what we most care about.

An amazing example of how we humans have polarised perceptions and points of view, is a recent comment made by the wife of a Russian academic working in London. She had just been to her hairdresser in the countryside. Her hairdresser had said she was really looking forward to a month long trip to Goa. The point the academic's wife made was "how it is the world is so un-equal that a hairdresser in the

UK can spend a month's holiday in Goa and the hairdresser in Goa cannot spend a month in the UK?"

Fair comment, would you agree?

While my reasoning is that she was a right fucking jealous cow (pardon my French), smartly pretending to hide her pain of unsatisfaction and her crushed ego and possibly in need of a holiday or in need of boosting her prestige (take your pick). The wifie's social status was diminished by the ability of the hairdresser! Not the pretentious wife of an academic? Apologies for my verbal diarrhea here, but seriously, do you honestly believe that by the talk I'll share later, people fail to see your true you?

You are right.

The majority do.

It took for me to write this book to understand what has actually happened. At the time I was simply confused as to why she would analyse it rather than be happy for her hairdresser.

And! Oh yes, your hypocritical author thought, what's your problem, wifie? Get a life of your own. But then that's me, the prejudices I'm still to deal with against women who behave, and they slavishly do, as though they sacrifice their lives for the success of their husbands. Or visa versa of course, the same is applicable to guys should the roles switch. It is more about my attachment of the label 'brainless slave' to them.

Do you know why? The easiest thing you can do in your life is to become a slave. It is easy. No responsibilities whatsoever. No challenges. You sit in life's cinema seat and enjoy the others going through life. Watching others taking the hits and humiliation as they stumble from one year of their life to the next. Of course you can get punished, but on a good day you get a treat or two by simply throwing in a complement or making your master feel guilty. We've all done that. We all are good at that. We practically mastered it during our childhood.

Explain me, what's the difference here between the wifie and those on benefits?

…no need. The supplier is different. At least in a direct food chain.

Let's get back to our wifie. Her remark regarding the difference in the hairdressers' pay.

On a first look her comment sounds quite legitimate and the feeling of how 'dare we' to enjoy our life when other people can't.

True, right?!

Now look at it from a different angle. How dare they have such cheap costs of living when it costs us so much to rent a 'hole' in London? My old *writing flat* rent in London cost me nearly two grand a month! And you should see the size of that thing.

How dare they eat a plate of rice for few cents in a cafe when we have to pay on average about £5 for a plate of rice as a side dish?

Valid argument, wouldn't you agree again?

Now here is a different option completely. Why do you base the richness of life or the richness of experience on behalf of another human being? How do you know, that in fact that is exactly that the hairdresser from Goa wants? It just may be, that in Goa the hairdresser is respected and has a loving family and children to look after or a family event to look

forward or a religious celebration she or he wants to participate in. Why do you think that your point of view is the one
that's correct?

I once asked my parents whether they'd ever consider moving abroad. They looked surprised, why would they need to
even consider moving anywhere. They'd never even thought
of that. Few days later, my dad said: "everyone knows us
here, we are respected. Why on earth would we want to
become nobodies in the foreign land?"

On the other hand, the words of my first husband regarding
Brazilians living in favellas are forever in my ears:

"Don't! Don't feel pity for them! They are much much
happier than you think they are. They want to be poor and
complain about the rich people because they want to be lazy
and enjoy the simple life."

That was his comment regarding my shock when I saw the
conditions people of favelas in Rio live in. Who was I to
argue with a guy who lived most of his life in Brazil.

Yes, I can hear you completely disagreeing with him, he who
has lived for 15 years in Brazil and was absolutely in love
with the country and he has provided many of the residents
with generously paid jobs because he believed people should
be rewarded generously. However, if you have never experienced the complete poverty, and by that I mean the meaning
of 'poverty' we have nowadays in the western world.

Let me share with you two examples of my poverty which are
still the most vivid in my memory. Mind you, I had no clue
during my first experience – that was the *poverty*.

When I was very very small and I was living in a small village
in the Ural Mountains region, separated from my father and
my mother, we had no hot water. In order to shower we had

to cut trees and to heat the Russian banya which is a separate minuscular building in the middle of the street or a garden area. During winter times we had to walk across -40 degree 'fresh' air in order to even start heating it up. Should we be slightly careless, we'd touch the banya's ceiling (the building was so small that you could not stand up fully inside) you'd get all the soot on you and would have to start all over again - providing we had enough warm water left. If not, we'd go back to our room (literally a room inside one building) in the cold and just accept we've messed it up. We then wait for a week or two till we get another opportunity to heat up the banya.

Banya is a Russian type of Sauna and was the only way to clean yourself many years ago. The buildings back then had no direct water supply.

The toilet was one per family or per community and it was in the middle of the street or in the middle of nowhere. Usually with holes eaten by worms during spring and autumn times.

Bread was only delivered once a week to our village and you could only purchase one loaf per person queuing. I still remember that being the smallest and the most useless creature by the village standards, I'd be the one to queue and if my relatives were lucky, they'd skip their jobs for a few minutes, risking being named and shamed for falling into a capitalistic trap and joining me just in time so we'd get enough bread for a week.

Before I share my next poverty story, I want to comment on this first one. I had no clue we were poor! The amount of excitement I'd get from standing up in line and knowing my life was important to my community was priceless! That feeling of being a little human being with my own rights and obligations was very empowering. The fact that if we'd got enough bread and my aunt got some fresh milk from a neighbour, it would be the equivalent of me buying diamond earring nowadays! I swear.

And not just diamond earrings but at least D/IF and minimum two carat each!

And most importantly if you re-read the wifie's comment again, you'll realise that the comment of the wife of Russian academic is based on a MATERIALISTIC understanding of the world. Completely ignoring our spirituality.

I mean, seriously? Do we completely ignore everything fundamental to our existence? We've replaced our lust for life, our appreciation of life's basic survival in exchange for over-hoarding in every aspect of our life.

Basic needs which are no longer basic.

We hoard what satisfies our hunger, we hoard what satisfies our need to feel warm, we hoard what satisfies the thirst, we now improve by hoarding even emotions.

And forget the vitamins, sex is a new type of hoarding!

Playing video games is a new type of hoarding.

Not speaking to your parents but staying in touch with your facebook and twitter buddies throughout the family dinner is the new type of social-hoarding.

Hoarding is another unrecognised form of mental health issue.

Never mind the children who are the key social-hoarders nowadays. I was recently enjoying some pancakes in Nantes in France. As I ate I observed a child excitedly sharing his thoughts about his weekend's activities with his mother. Whilst the boy's excitement grew his mother took out her iphone from her handbag and started playing solitaire!

After few minutes of hesitation, the clever child decided to join in the game so he still felt as though they were together.

Wake up. It is no longer about protecting ourselves non-stop from what can and can't possibly happen. Yes, there is starvation in some areas yet there is overeating in others. But it is not by constantly providing that you'll help the others but with setting yourself as an example. And your needs are not really, not anymore, what your life is about. Just like with children.

Have you ever washed dishes with a sponge? You put some liquid soap on it, you scrub the plates, you squeeze the sponge and... once you bring the sponge next to the water tap, the sponge extraordinary fast, sucks all the water it can possibly handle in, spilling and all, but nevertheless it sucks in so much water it is really impressive. Give the sponge to your children and let them play with water, they'll be amused for quite some time.

The sponge here is a metaphor for your child. A child is like a sponge, hungry to suck in any information they can, the child repeats your words, the child repeats your behaviour and... the child repeats your thoughts and excuse my frankness, shitty or aggressive language, should you use any. Quite often I've seen parents amusing themselves when a three year old suddenly picks up rather vulgar swearing and begins repeating it.

Naturally, later you will explain to your child the word is not to be used in public etc etc, but the damage is done.

When running workshops for Westminster Council for parents, I particularly addressed the fact that many parents aren't aware or to be more accurate, they ignore the fact the child is able to think. The child is not just thinking but over-thinking at times as well. This is how, although you mean well, you have already programmed your child towards failure and anxieties. Of course you do not think you do, all that money you spend on the best education, all the efforts you make to buy the right books.

What matters are your own thoughts and the patterns of behaviour around your child, especially during their early age until their first few years through school.

It is because they still don't have an opportunity to build their own self-preservation mechanisms, they copy yours. It may not appear that way, because they are not capable of copying you completely. These traits are 'copied' by being translated into their heads or their current perception of the world. Although they are not capable of digesting or translating in that moment, the information, your thoughts and your body signals, are safely stored in their little heads. Once their brain or perceptions develop to the level of understanding they'll use yours, they'll use your cues, your words, your patterns of behaviours.

Luckily the majority will rebel against certain patterns of your behaviour because with age they manage to learn and recognise that some of your patterns of behaviour are wrong and in fact are attracting the wrong results.

You are not robots, yet should you take the responsibility to bring a child into the world, it is *your* responsibility to create the world. To give the most happiness and being blunt, the most inspirational environment for a child to grow.

In the end – it is you who wins and wins big. Firstly you support your child in an enriching developmental environment, secondly – it is your opportunity to switch your attention away from your old and highly destroying habits and direct it towards the goals or experiences you seek or have been always wanted.

No I am not from a La-La land. We still have jobs or which-ever ways we learn to sustain our food supplies, and our basic needs. I am even offering you a bizarrely odd yet crystal clear solution: you simply stop wasting your time on the negative thoughts, unnecessary behavioural habits such as hoarding and addictions, and unnecessary anger for in fact they got you NOWHERE! Switch your attention to a more fulfilling use of your spare time.

Before you try to tell me – what spare time?

I'll say…

The time you go to sleep, instead of relaxing you'll grind those anger emotions towards someone.

The time you sit at work in front of your computer and all you think is how much you hate that fucking employee next to you.

The time, you are out with your friends for a fun time and all you do is complain about your bitch girlfriend or that asshole ex of yours.

The time you sit on public transport and all you can think of is why on earth that child won't shut up.

The time you want to watch TV and start complaining there is nothing to watch.

It is almost as if you constantly seek something to complain about, be angry about, be unsatisfied about.

And the child absorbs it all. Just like that sponge…

8

Communication in relationships

*B*e a connoisseur of the people you really let into your life."

Let's presume you are not so poor that you can afford to spend some time with those around you rather than working away to make ends meet. Let's also, for accessibility of the argument, presume you are not of a generation where you work hard to ensure your child misses nothing in life as you did, while their children or grandchildren most likely will. For your children do not have the same beliefs as you do and may well detest the hard work of yours when they miss your physical and spiritual presence in their life. Balance is not something we are familiar with and it costs us dearly should we fail to achieve it.

You are likely to have many friends and you socialise regularly. You collaborate. Be that in a work environment or your family. You are happy to collaborate and participate. A beautiful example here would be the play 'Abigail's Party'.

The play beautifully portrays, in an extreme manner naturally, our desire to be superior, no matter what.

While we do not realise it consciously, we fight day and night for our beliefs to be imposed onto others. Partially because, as we've discovered earlier, of our fears and by degree due to our habits and upbringing. Should anything go wrong, the other side, party, call it whatever you want is to blame. In work and in our personal life we take relationships as given. We take collaboration as given.

Why would anyone in healthy state of mind take to collaborate or any type of relationship as given? It does take time to develop any relationship, does it not?

Yes, you can hit it off at once, be that with a potential sexual partner, a potential business partner, with the child you wish to adopt. So far, it is not about agreeing with each other points of view, it is about enriching each others' life. It is about cultivating imagination and awakening the true potential and internal knowledge in each party. And in such a way that the knowledge, experience or the information is of added value, not of similar value, for there is simply no interest in that. You may just as simply be at home and enjoy yourself with a glass of the most disgusting wine yet imagining it is a great wine and persuading yourself you are right. That is a self-centered and a limited if not degenerative approach.

Just ask yourself, how it is you know that this glass of wine is the best? For those who are not wine connoisseurs, choose what you think you have an excellent taste in. For example you understand about music, art or the best holidays locations, or simply which car engine is the best and apply to my example.

It is normal that when you decide you are good enough at something or you wish to become good at something, the main purpose behind is to have a better and more satisfying experience. As well as becoming respected for your knowledge and expertise, ie you have an opportunity to be important and indulge yourself in being respected for whatever reason.

Peer recognition is still among the highest priorities, in fact in many cases, you will agree, recognition is even more important than food or clothes. That is usually the main purpose and don't be a smart ass here for you can be honest, no one is speaking to you – you are just reading this book. For all you know, I could be very wrong, or at least you choose to disagree with me because you are not ready to be honest with yourself.

That is fine. Stick to your opinion and consider there are people like this that you know and you can accept this point of view if you think as one of those (others) pretentious people. Because you are 100 percent flawless.

There you go, you decided to challenge your expertise by either joining debate clubs or wine tasting courses where you hope to learn something new, yet you discover that the wine expert in fact has less knowledge and experience than you have. It is a bit like talking to an Italian, where he or she claims that the best bakery in the whole world is located in this particular street in Rome, and if you question a bit further you'll discover that rather conveniently that best bakery in the world is simply located next to his house. Or it is like talking to a Russian, where the strongest and the cleverest nation is the world is in fact Russia. And if you try to challenge such seemingly limited view, Russians even have an answer:

"Well of course we are the smartest nation on earth because we are Euroasians, so we combine the knowledge and 'brain' of the western and eastern worlds together."

Now back to our wine example. There you are, you have finished the wine course, you stuck up on some hugely recognised brands as well as mixed it up with your own choices and – voilà – you will start your talk with the wine everyone knows or at least read that everyone states it is the best wine, and then you pour the cheap wine and explain why it is great if not even better than the bottle you've mentioned earlier. If you guests try and like it, that will re-affirm your expert knowledge and you'll continue considering yourself an expert.

Now that is a self-indulging concept.

Here is another enriching concept. You believe your wine is the best but you are open to the opportunity there can be better and you find a buddy expert and you each bring a bottle of wine and you both taste your own and each other's wine and your compare or share your experiences. You'll find out why one wine is better than another or why both are great and what makes them special - or you simply decide you need to try more similar wines because you are not 100 percent convinced that is the top wine.

Or like with cars, yes the engine must be better, but it is not until you drive and test it that you form an opinion of your own and it is only when others point out other benefits and explain to you why the most respected politicians or gangsters will go for another car that you'll be happy to switch your opinion. Should the people mentioned to you be aspirational (to you) figures.

What I am trying to say here is that your opinion is really never ever 100 percent your own, because that is what experience and collaboration is all about. It is ever continuous and fluid (yes with bumps and hits at times, but ideally a fluid) process. It is never about who is right or wrong, it is about discussing the matter or a subject in a sense that you come up with the seemingly best decision at any given time, recognising that that solution or agreement is only correct at this time and it may be well wrong in the near future once you learn alternative experiences.

I was really privileged to meet this girl, let's call her Ann (that is not her real name). Ann came on board to explore the possibility of delivering my messages in multidimensional ways. Via video production and other resources. What struck me about her was the fact she never took my 'NO' as no. Yes, if you worked with me you'd know my explanation that 'NO' is never a no and it may be just that the person is busy or there is another priority at that moment in time. Or it simply could be that at this time they already purchased a similar service or a product from somewhere else.

However, I did not realise I am still using 'NO' myself. I only got it when Ann, suddenly and completely unexpectedly, to my 'NO', looked at me, paused for a few seconds and as though I've never ever said 'NO' to her, she put forward the very same idea in different words.

It was as though she has translated 'NO' as 'I don't understand what you are trying to say'. In fact that very moment I had an idea running through my confused and overloaded brain. I simply wanted to register it. Sadly, Ann's comment caught me off guard and I'll never know for sure what that idea was, however, the fact that she did deliver her idea eventually to me has resulted in our collaboration.

Did we always agree? No. But what we did learn was that it is no longer about agreeing or disagreeing – it is about complementing and developing ideas further til we feel it's right to be presented to the general public or a particular business depending on the project we were working on.

Yes collaboration is not about yes or no, but con-tin-u-ous processes, where ideas can only become polished by seeing different angles of the solution you are working towards. As I have just read in one of the reviews of my dear Alex Clark and his co-author book *Linguistic Nativism and the Poverty of the Stimulus*: "It can be in fact a dizzying array of facts and new information". A dizzying array indeed.

What do you do in this case? You stick to the rule 20-80.

As long as you've got 20 percent of the information or a decision you strongly agree with – you go ahead. Why? Because any decision you may find will be only right for NOW, possibly in the nearest future additionally, and if you are very very lucky in the distant future as well. But as experience evolves and more information comes to surface, the more there will be a need to change or suggest a new solution.

Compare it to school books. You learn one piece of information, then your child comes home and tells you your knowledge is false for there are new discoveries. In fact zero is no longer zero and the value now depends on the context you are using it in?!

Or if giving a completely bizarre example, than you'd say $1+1=2$, yet if we talk about sex and producing an offspring, where 1 is one human and another 1 is another human, the fact that $1+1=$ is definitely not 2 should the result of impregnating be successful, it could be $=3$ in case of one child and it could be $=4$ in case of twins and so on.

Yes, I understand the absurdity of that example, I am just trying to give you a different point of view, or a different way to perceive things.

Nothing is still, nothing is permanent. Life is fluid, relationships are fluid and collaborations are in fact, should you accept that perception is quite different for every individual – fluid. And that is the TRUE BEAUTY of it. Because life is about experiencing and interaction and SHARING. Sharing knowledge, experience or opinion.

And while I will agree with you that in relationship one can out-grow the other person and you decide to go different ways, but look at it this way. If your emotional connection is still high, there may be, just maybe a possibility that you want to learn and consider the other point of view, rather than just saying no.

Hopefully one of you is more spiritually developed (I do mean more spiritually developed for it is not about being an idiot or a smart person, for we are more multi-faceted than that perfectly cut diamond). Instead of saying no, put it differently and ask directly and honestly: "Why do you believe your point is correct, and what's in it for me?"

Yes, simply and bluntly. It just may be that the person may open up and give you a different perspective to whatever you were arguing or disagreeing about. Or it may be you will find a common ground to agree on while disagreeing on other points.

Naturally if it's still definitely against your beliefs or needs at any given time, there is a possibility you'll need to withdraw, resign or break up your relationship. Perhaps even send a poor child to your grandparents while you take your time to think about the upcoming break up or possibility to resign from your position.

Conversely, never ever follow something you are forced to agree with, while the other person or a child or your business partner is right 100 percent, it may be that your way is also correct and you simply need to find another environment or people in order to deliver what you want or what you believe in.

The experience is never singular and unanimous. Quite the opposite it can be that this wine is absolutely the best for you and yes that is the most respected château, yet if I absolutely hate it – I either didn't have enough time to acquire the taste, or I do in fact absolutely hate it.

It is like in that movie *Runaway Bride* with Julia Roberts as the main actress, where she cooks every single type of egg, poached, omelet, scrambled and eats each of them in order to work out which is the way SHE prefers.

The majority of successful people who are respected and admired have something in common. They DO listen to others before making up their mind. It is common to them to investigate and find out other points of view on a subject. They tend to consider others, involve them, as well as those who are going to be responsible. And most importantly they understand the value of trust. It starts with trust, before anyone is even willing to consider (out of the good will) your point of view or your suggestion. I love the saying:

"Trust reduces transaction costs" It does indeed.

Many believe they really control everything around them. Alas, that is not even close to the reality. In fact they may believe so when in fact they are acting out the desires of those around them. Remember the saying:

"Behind every great man there's a great woman"

How many times in order to get a payrise or a favour, have you first built trust with the next responsible person, to put a good word in for you so to speak?

We are far from the ideal rationalising human being that we would prefer to be. Partially, this is because we do not consist purely of our mind. Yet due to a lack of self control mentally, emotionally and for many physically we tend to be self-deceptive. We daydream and live a lazy and overconfident existence, contrary to what many say.

Declaring that while half of the population is lacking confidence, the other is overly confident would not be far from reality. One way or another, we can be diagnosed as ill - again.

9

Fear of the unknown

With all other pathologies we experience, the most paradoxical one is a fear of the unknown.

Let's face it, the 'unknown' is pretty much anything. Anyone working in the financial market is more or less aware of that.

You do not know for sure tomorrow will or will not rain.

You do not know for sure that that house will stay in a family for another 20 years.

You do not know for sure you'll stay together forever.

You expect it to be so. Yet you do not know.

'Expectations' succeed at fooling us rather well, because we saw it happen already.

Even if it won't be so in our individual cases, at least the expecting reduces plenty of unnecessary anxieties, until the unexpected happens. Then all hell breaks loose.

Yet for the majority we *know* and we *expect to expect*. Anything new, untested, untold, unknown and unexpected is therefore a bloodcurdling spooky hairy monster.

And based on our wisdom, any changes can cause just that – a meeting with hair-raising effects. As a matter of fact anything that we do not know presents us with a potential heart attack and possibly dire death.

Years ago, when I started running confidence workshops, my workshops began with a description of fear as false evidence appearing to be real. I would then go on to tell a story of how many conquered their fears or at least reduced them to a sufferable level have later recognised their fears where foolish.

Now, I've learnt to put my clients through *making mistakes*.

I jokingly state your life is like dating. You want to believe that the less desired *selection* would reject you and as often as possible, so you learn the best possible skills you need to *get it right* when the suitable opportunity strikes. The pain you go through when getting things wrong and the challenges you meet to conquer the fear you face every time, helps you build the ample stamina that you ought to have in life. It even attempts to produce a much deeper and profound result then many expect.

As you get better at making mistakes and facing your fears, your own newly gathered cues which become so deep-seated, the desired results, be that meeting the right people, the dream partner or simply getting the right help, are almost drawn to you.

Your subconscious is now as a switched on light bulb, radiating your signals outwards. The others' subconscious responds. Whether they want it to or not. Yet, given the fact our subconscious is in a more harmonious state than our mind chatter, it only helps us and everyone involved on the path.

Once in a while to rebuild such valuable tools, all you need is to change environment. It seems very difficult to succeed in reaching your desired outcomes. You question whether the world is in fact really against you. Not so much in opposition to you as your cultural traditions may not support your new beliefs. On the other hand, as your subconscious affects those around you, the same happens to you.

We are not training our mental and emotional parts in our schools. At best, you will have read some self-help books and then forgot all about them, or eagerly thrown yourself into one discipline after another without noticing any long term changes. Short splashes of energy boosts and *happy* feelings – yes, long-term, probably unlikely.

Mental and emotional discipline is simply not considered to be crucial. **Yet it is essential**.

If you remain in the same environment you will be always be subjected to the same influences unless you are strong enough to implement the very first changes yourself. If you are faint, surrounding your friends and family this would subdue your cravings for change, or restrict any of the changes from happening.

Life does not go on unchanged. Life is fluid. Life is movement. Changes are inevitable. You change. You are not the same as you where 20 years ago. Your relationships with others are not the same. You more likely to wear a different clothing size now than 20-30 years ago.

Admittedly some changes take time and give you an opportunity to prepare and in some cases you don't even notice the process. Just one day you wake up and notice that your daughter is no longer a child. Some transformations are almost instant and catch you off guard, causing you lots of distress and illness in some cases.

Partially it is due to the disease I call 'stagnant nine to five'. Most of our lives we are programmed by our parents and society that our whole life purpose is to get good grades and a secure job. Possibly get married and to have children.

After that we are lost and we jump at our children – brain-washing them with the same tales we were told earlier in our lives. We hate that, but because we are scared we follow the traditions. Until and if something stirs up our 'stagnant nine to five' which let's be honest isn't that common after all.

We'd rather stay unsatisfied and complain than do some-thing about it. We'd rather stay unhappy in a marriage than face the public humiliation of being single (more for women than males). We'd rather bad mouth our colleagues than explore another opportunity. Yet in most cases it's about continual exploration of opportunities.

When you lead a pretty much-established lifestyle, life around you evolves. I do also refer here to those who do not work nine to five or consider themselves successful. Life revolves around work, regular trips and holidays and whatev-er else considered the regular stuff to do.

You are not just a physical body. It really is not the only part of you, you need to take care of or obsessively train the other parts too.

Lately my favorite park, Regents Park is no longer safe for walking, there are more runners then people trying to relax and peacefully take in their surroundings. If a dog doesn't get you – a runner will. Jokes aside, your mind and your emo-tions (yes, I know, if you belong to what you call 'above middle class' you do not have them, emotions are for the poor) also need evolution and training.

Add to it soul nourishment which goes in addition to your physical body, mind and emotions and you get the picture that for the most part of your life, you really only took care suitably (if you actually did) of your physical self. The part of you that is responsible for drinking, eating, reproducing. I bet at least one or two of your other parts are completely undeveloped, be that emotional, mind or your spiritual side. When I say spiritual, I do not refer to any religious believes here. That is the main cause for your fears. You are like a child who saw a large furry dog barking and got scared due to misinterpreting the 'excited to see you' bark projected by the dog for 'I am going to eat you'.

10

Rich us, poor them

If you've read my other books or attended my workshops, you'll know that I've spent two years of my life working and living between London and LA.

English and Americas are already two different cultures. And LA is different to the whole of the USA. Now here is something you cannot disagree with. Purely because is my own experience and it is absolutely true to me.

You, on the other hand, can form a different opinion but you cannot argue with something my subconscious mind has produced and presented to me.

While I was busy working, shagging, partying, supervising at work, overseeing the whole production, drinking cocktails, making even more sales, visiting strip clubs, dining at low class diners topped up with entertainment at the best LA restaurants and nightclubs... my subconscious mind was working non-stop. It observed, collected data, processed it, re-directed it to different compartments of my brain and then withdrew the content of the very same compartments, added more data to it and restructured it again. That was absolutely non-stop and during that time I was running on two to four hours of sleep.

I have visited The States many times since. I have spent time with the world's most notorious desperate housewives in The Hamptons.

I've been entertained by the brutal and far more straightforward than etiquette requires Jews of NY (yes, there is such thing). I've spend some time in la-la land Boulder, where I once while shopping for some books had to step aside for one of the local residents has remembered he was late for his psychic reading appointment and he nearly swept me of my feet, sadly not in the romantic Hollywood way I would have preferred.

And a few more trips, yes including the famous Berkley where you are not allowed to sell any crap unless you price it at least three times higher than anywhere else in the USA; and including San. Francisco where flirting with hot looking males was, as politely put by my prince charming, barking up the wrong tree.

It was only during a dinner that I was invited to with my brainiac Mr Charming and a French couple who had freshly immigrated to Maryland for their scientific work that I realised how my sweet and hard working subconscious brain has been working so hard during the last 10 years.

I had produced a whole account on Americans without consciously realising that in fact a product of my brain, which for a rare moment was directly delivered via my tongue.

Apparently my subconscious has given me the facts any tourist guide writer would cheer at. Americans, I was loudly and cheerfully announcing to the freshly immigrated French couple, are... well... everything is extreme. While it's really hot outside and you have the whole shower off your seat dripping down your spine and your legs, should you enter a mall or in fact any premises where you really want to chill, you'll chill. Extremely fast. Because it is more likely than not it'll be in the presence of a fridge friendly temperature.

Should you visit the USA during the winter months, you're more than guaranteed to experience a tropical weather inside the premises.

Looking for an upper middle class or a more salubrious area to live? Follow the American extreme nature. Basically look for the slimmest looking population. They'll probably be a very boring crowd because between their working hours and extreme sports routines, they hardly have anything else on their mind til someone else introduces a new status sustain 'game'. You can bet – it'll be another extreme.

On another visit to the East Coast while I was dining in one of the upper-middle class suburban areas, the restaurant owner went on and on about how fresh their vegetables are. I provoked the owner by genuinely complementing him on their tasty salad.

Big mistake.

The owner gave me a big American smile and reeled off what seemed to be a carefully rehearsed presentation on how his farmers pick the vegetables fresh in the morning and his goal is to deliver it to our table by the evening. I restrained my laughter but burst out once he had retreated in the kitchen. If that's organic then my childhood of eating vege- tables straight from the garden patch out of desperation was an organic diet indeed? Hah?

It almost epitomises the upper class status today, to live as Tuscan peasants!

So are Americans alone in their extremities? We are all a small step away sadly. As for our earlier mentioned French hosts? They pointed out, their French relatives are eager to visit NY. I'm sure they will be greeted with disappointment as their expectations are based on the images portrayed on the silver screen and manipulated by Hollywood.

We are so disrupted in our natural cue production that we can't trust our own subconscious to produce us with the (yes temporary, because it does get adjusted constantly) map of the world. We completely ignore the fact the social skills are to be learned and developed by ourselves, we trust completely in the books we read and the movies we watch!

No wonder with such seemingly progressive technology, our brains are heading towards severe degradation. We are ill.

All of us.

We are ill or mentally disturbed in one way or another.

We are not handling progress and changes well. Our education system nor our social system nor our work environment supports progress and change!

A few do, but due to their limited numbers, their work is getting lost amidst our capitalistic minds which blindly and stupidly believe that just because we start following Eastern dogmas or regularly take a yoga class we are automatically better than others. Actually you are more stupid than others. Why? Because you rely on your brain to relax as you take anything you need as an explanation from very outdated rules and traditions.

It is time to wake up. Progress can be fast. The world moves fast. The changes are fast. And with that, the separation between classes (yes we still have them, now just relax and deal with that) and cultures and countries are growing.

While most of you seek solutions through a new improved social or communist ways – you are seriously fucked up in your head. It does not work. If that worked, Russia would be much better off than the rest of the world, but it's not. The idea is based on financial distribution and is completely absurd because you concentrate on substance and not skills. You think of satisfying the physical and not the all human aspects. You feed the greed and provoke the violence.

Education and teaching people to work on different aspects of self and accumulate the knowledge at much faster rate is a new way.

Why? Simply because if you give a poor man a thousand pounds, they'll be poor again in a week or so. You forget the fact the poor are not educated about money, how to handle it, what to do with it. The Robin Hood idea was working before (if it ever was), but not anymore.

There is a reason we have such a growing gap between chavs and upper middle class in England. Middle class? If anything they are the struggling middle class and then there is a gap. Emptiness.

If you think that the rich should share, why? So that the poor burn the wealth for their instantaneous pleasure culture? What's the point in that?

There is a need to educate the lower classes and build an understanding that it is in their interests to achieve, to learn and to explore.

I once attended a big conference where the presenters were surprisingly honest. The conference was predominantly (apart from me basically) black. Blacks living in England, predominantly recently emigrated from Africa or born in England with ancestral roots in Africa. They discussed how they had organised free education and free resources for the

Lambeth council and similar communities yet no one had turned up. They have made such an effort to provide help. They had organised great speakers, they had found sponsors. No one has turned up. They were in total disbelief. They were hoping to help youngsters, strengthen the communities and assist those who are in need of financial or educational help. They were hoping to help single parents.

The atrophy of the brains of those we think need help, have moved away from thinking "How can I achieve X" to the way of thinking "How shall I steal from X"? Hah?

It is almost as though the 'poor' population have developed a ridiculous feeling of over-entitlement.

This reminds me of Russians in the early ages in Germany when they wanted anything and Germans would say no to their benefit-claims; all they had to do was to call them Fascists. It worked. The national guilt feeling for something they no longer have a connection with still grips the national image in fear.

It is the same with England. It is a country where people have such a huge amount of guilt. Guilt with money. Guilt that they have money that it is uncommon for a humble teacher to die and donate her multimillion pound fortune. No one would ever have suspected she would have left a lone gift to another greedy and lucky charity.

It is the same with England – the financial guilt is producing a system that feeds the over entitlement of the uneducated youngsters.

It is even more inspiring to see the city bankers who may well come from a similar upbringing but are making it through. To see how they'll do anything to support their families so they look good in everyone's eyes, yet to my question what should we do to inspire the new generation to appreciate knowledge and skills?

The bankers respond: "Who cares? Leave them as they are. I've made it, so can they."

Yes they can, providing the pain threshold is raised by not giving so much for free without them giving something back to the community. There is enough 'dead load' of human flesh. Those who simply get a degree, get married, reproduce an offspring and then stick to the chores of sustaining whatever image they aspired to, be that middle class, upper middle class, white trash or the cool hipsters.

What people need to be given is more responsibility.

And people want it. Rather than trying to feel their need and desire of being part of society by feeding them financially or with their labour unnecessary charity organisations (oh, c'mon! It's not a secret that institutions like Sotheby's and alike have whole courses on how to save money by creating the very charity organisations) but by actual responsibility.

For example, voting. Why is it not obligatory? We all know how everyone is absolutely smart enough to criticise the government of his or her own country.

Not so long ago I witnessed once again, a respectable celebrity couple complaining about social injustices and new 'ridiculous' government policies from the comfort of their sofa and sipping a glass of wine. The debate had escalated and at its peak moment of almost shouting at the TV with their views, I calmly interjected asking the purpose of their stressed out state? They redirected their aggression towards me. I stopped them at once and said, oh I do agree, but the government does not know your real views because you keep them to yourselves. Everyone is suddenly brave behind the closed doors. No communication effort needed.

Yes, we rightly find ways of cohabiting with the minimum stress to ourselves. Yet if you have some brain mass left and you are not one of those Japanese women who pretends to be an upper class English by making sure her accent sounds slightly confusing next to her strong Asian features and doing everything in her powers just to sustain that 'status', then it is about time we simply open the debate.

It is not a bad idea to try some collective votes. Of course the outcome will be wrong, because the majority of us are uneducated! Pardon me, we are educated, it is deeper – we are not AWARE! But it's better we make more mistakes now than later.

I've been brought up with one relative openly hating Americans, actually it is very common for the older generation of Russians. If you ask them why, they will have no constructive reply ready because in fact they do not hate Americans, but they think they do due to the post-communist echos. Another relative of mine would make me swear to understand that blacks are blacks because they do not have soap, even though it distressed me and made me cry.

Another relative once stated, he would shoot every single gay person on the face of the earth should he get hold of enough of an arsenal.

If you read that and your anger builds and blood boils up, relax. My relatives are as ignorant as you. Purely because we prefer to live in a carefully constructed bubble and do everything possible to protect it from breaking its shell. We hate change. We hate any change.

Alas, it is no longer avoidable.

I mean if anything, my upbringing should really produce another bitch with the expectation of constant over-entitlement. It is purely down to my life experiences and a travel bag and extreme nature that I see the other side of people.

If you think I am not hurt by being diminished by so many people – I am *no longer* only now. I did suffer internally and I have no clue how I managed not to bend in order to please others and make my life much easier.

I honestly suspect that it is due to my childhood which gave me so much hell that anything that has happened after I ran away from my home was absolutely nothing next to the 24/7 fear of being raped, robbed, beaten up on the street and/or psychologically abused at home. I was living on egg shells for most of my childhood, what came next was more of an uneven road surface with occasional dips, probably too many dips.

The fact that I am welcome in any social circle gives me an opportunity to be an insider and an outsider in any circle - think Camilla, Duchess of Cornwall.

Yet such a discourse in my social position lets me stay, as much as possible, free from social status boundaries.

I have to be honest, it is long ago I learned my value and I've made sure I've put my skills and my advantages to good use at any given opportunity. There is no point in pretending and then regretting, there is much more to acknowledging, living and experiencing. There is no point in finding yet another way to diagnose to your Mental Health Issue. There is a point in dealing with life obstacles and enjoying the better things it has to offer.

I invite you to join me and others. Life is fun. Much more fun than you ever realised before x

PART 3

Additional chapters, For true seekers.

11

Interconnectivity

Newspaper headlines demand that the government create more jobs and it seems that election campaigns may depend entirely on that.

But if you simply stroll across to Washington DC or just take the underground you will clearly see that the jobs to be offered are not the solution at all.

Firstly the jobs which are required to be created are not the ones which will cover the bills, hence what's the point in work when it simply isn't enough.

On the other hand – many people DO NOT WANT to work! Especially when there is an opportunity to complain, blame the government and observe those who earn more from their misfortune, those who work do not give them enough money so they can definitely not work.

While University campuses and newspapers are bombarding us with headlines about jobs, the government is trying to create jobs. It is a paradox at its best.

Let's examine the subject. Firstly and most importantly, people are not educated or brought up to a level of seeing life as an opportunity to experience. Most people see life as drag.

Once upon a time it was easier to cut the ailing tree and plant new seeds. It is time we look into planting the new seeds. Logically as humans no one is even suggesting cutting the old trees, we focus on heritage and history.

Now just may be the time when people need to start teaching themselves and installing the resources to educate a younger generation. The jobs are there and it appears there are simply not enough qualified and educated people to fill the roles.

We are dreaming of exploring other outer spaces and galaxies – when we fail to communicate among ourselves. When we lack basic knowledge in our immediate environments.

I used to say that higher education is not important, until very recently, until I start writing this book. But with closer observation and studying our ill society further, I say you need both street and higher education.

Our society, contrary to what we want to believe in or read in the press is extremely isolated. Certain layers of people with a particular pedigree more often than not will apply for some form of higher education. The majority of the poorer population will try to get the opportunity to give their kids more stable life, ie where they can earn money with their hands rather than their heads.

Firstly and most importantly for such a social layer, it is this fact that will keep supporting their belief.

"If you want to earn honest money you have to work hard".

Fundamentally, rubbing into their children's noses their own failures. And in addition without even realising it they create children who are poorly equipped for life. We need to develop our brains as fast as our hands. The progress of technology is not creeping up on us but leaping across the globe with giant steps. As a result this advance leaves many uneducated people without jobs. Remember the British Coal Miners? Where are they now?

However, the same applies to the children of well-off parents. As you develop your brain, you need to develop your life awareness. It is all good to know what MA stands for, but what good is it to you should you get kidnapped during your trip in Mexico?

Yes, it is an extreme case. But the MONEY that the poor keep dreaming of inheriting, robbing, winning the lottery or saving up till the day they die will not save them and they'll be still in debts.

MONEY that the rich are trying hard to protect or spend or earn or all of that simultaneously IT IS NOT EVERYTHING! Our relationships with others and our communication skills as well as how we interact with others – this is EVERYTHING.

Acquire those capabilities and skills and money will be just another aspect of life, possibly a very positive one as well.

While MONEY took on a life of it's own from the initially intended purpose; or possibly it was never an intended purpose in the first place and actually it is possible that MONEY was created as a separate entity to control, aspire and underline wealth. It's the communications and relationships with others that drive the world.

Drive your life. Drive your lifestyle. And, drive the further flow of money IN or OUT of your life. Drive your life..Don't let the medical diagnosis drive your life.

Get both educations if you can. Get the missing education at your first opportunity. And get one thing straight, there is no one to be blamed for an unsatisfactory education which teaches us next to nothing apart from the system, and provides us with the feeling of over-entitlement.

We got our education and so what? Did you do anything about it? The chances are – not. Because be you in finance (where people are more educated or trained with military precision by the guard dogs on long term investments) or not, you also think short term. As long as you are not in school or education – you do not care. As long as you've managed to mentally drag (yes drag with drugging of course) your kids through the education – you do not care. You become as most of us become: we have got an education, NOW WHAT? If we do not get the job, we wait. If we cannot find the job according to our degree, we blame the system.

Why do you expect that the teachers, who are not well paid and are usually coming from the poorer population will support the prospering mentality, oh they keep saying to their students that they can achieve anything. But it is the teachers themselves who do not achieve many things and set themselves as an example to Johnny or Lizzy.

Is there any school which teaches children about the differences of communication? Is there any class in school teaching about cultural differences and what, how, when and anything related to that? There are psychology classes of course. Psychology classes which consist of collected knowledge but not real life experience and how to apply the theories.

Are there any classes explaining the few basic traits of behaviour and reasons behind bulling and violence?

Are there classes teaching about respecting your parents and your society yet it is your responsibility to make something of yourself and how it is you'll contribute to the society?

Are there classes explaining why sometimes people are happy living poor (yes, it is true and I've been poor and happy till I've been told otherwise) and why some people no matter how much of the material wealth they acquire they still stay unhappy? And that it is their own choice which weaknesses and addictions they decide to pursue?

Are there classes which educate the pupil they are owed nothing? The list can continue.

Regarding new recruits. You know those annoying young-sters, freshly educated, full of ideas, who know everything and think you are a dead weight in your own company? What about remembering yourself and offering this young-ster a one-off opportunity under any conditions you feel like. We all crave more recognition, we all crave more success. Let's just accept that.

It is our driving stimulus after all. Why not use it to our advantage? Of course in parts they are wrong, they lack the experience you have! However there is a great chance they have an idea you have not tried before.

Possibly they'll be happy to prove it to you at their own cost? And even if they fail – don't dishearten them, don't encour-age too much either, simply weigh all the elements that did work and that did not. When you support their ego – they'll reward you with their hard work and trust more than any other much higher paid employee.

It is like an interview. After an interview, people who keep their jobs though understand they'd like to earn more con-firm: but the director trusts me and I have responsibilities! Why not let them risk their own time, and hopefully not at any significant cost financially or time-wise to you, on ideas they think might work, providing they are ready to bear the consequences of failure?

You cannot deny the importance of feeling recognized not to yourself not to OTHERS. And you know what? We are all inter-connected.

Ever been in the presence of an angry person and felt really hostile towards others after interacting with them? Or have you ever been in a presence of a person who simply inspires you and 'lifts your spirits'?

There is such understanding as inter-connectivity. The moments of internal dialogues will cease to make sense with a more thorough understanding of inter-connection and the philosophy of 'all is one'.

As you read earlier, at times you simply do not know whether the emotions-thoughts-ideas are yours or if they belong to others: other people, your dog (in case you feel the need to feed the poor pooch), other entities or you may have a slight case of schizophrenia. Jokes aside, an understanding that some thoughts and desires are yours uniquely while they seemingly (could possibly) belong to someone else is due to the connectivity on a broader level. For example, the thought or desire is in fact yours and of no one else, yet it is along the lines of the bigger picture, bigger project if you like.

For example the whole community is working towards experiencing a new level of pleasure, you, on the other hand, completely unaware of the fact (or so you choose to think that you are unaware) come up with a new packaging for a juice brand, where a cute girl looks really happy while drinking the juice. Now 'the community' has an opportunity not just to drink the same juice, now it has an extra emotional added value. As you drink the juice you most probably feel as though you are happier.

Here, while you thought you had a very unique idea of coming up with a new packaging idea, the idea was supported by a community desire to have a richer experience.

It is like this with art. The Eiffel tower for example got lots of criticism. Why? It did not add emotional satisfaction. For whatever reason! Reason here is not important. The important fact is that the building did not produce the effect of added emotional value, or in other words it wasn't enriching emotionally compared to what other buildings and art Paris has. Similar effect was produced when the Modern Museum Art building has been completed.

Whenever you have a dialogue and you have what I call 'verbal diarrhea', whether discussing should you or shouldn't you, whether simply trying to analyze why did he or she did it to you - you switch on your rationality. And in doing so you switch off your connection. To imprint it in you quite literally I'll go into extreme measures by stating the harsh truth: you cancel or murder, yes murder any opportunity to have a direct experience.

In order to have a better understanding or knowledge or ideas or get the income you seek, you almost want to switch off your mind. Ideas are not something 'rationale' you acquire by analyzing, measuring, studying. Ideas are from your inner knowledge and experience.

Like with DNA, you may have a gene which causes abnormal cell growth, yet it is a radiation of certain power that needs to awaken that particular gene to stimulate the abnormal cell growth. Same with you. You have an inner knowledge, it is the interaction with certain people, community or entities that that idea is 'sparking' in your mind.

'Rationale' is what you use when you have the idea and now you want to find out how! In this material/physical world you can deliver it. Not the other way around.

It is easier once you grasp the complexity of our interactive mechanisms. You have an emotional level and a rational level. On an emotional level you have subcategories as your 'clean' emotions (as much as it is possible at all) and you have emotions of experiences. For example, the boss has fired you: "That bastard! I hate the boss for causing me emotional pain."

In a state like that you really let the 'experience' emotions overtake your own emotions which provide you with the BEST ideas based on your surroundings.

An example here would be: bastard made you lose your job. In 'rationale' state, you only go via experience emotions and keep blaming, complaining, slowly turning into feeling sorry for yourself leading to life disappointment and really hoping for luck that needed radiation, as with the case in DNA will spark off a new opportunity.

The word hope is a negative word, contrary to mass belief, since it means you are dependent. You are dependent on GOD, a neighbour or possibly a parent or parent or a god-like figure. Just before jumping fully to the hope explanation. Here is another example of direct experience or your own experience: where instead of blaming your boss - you do recognise the emotional pain it causes you. And! Here is the key! You choose the emotion you believe is best for you to experience. You can achieve it in a variety of ways - the basic example would be - body vs emotions exercise (bending down and shouting I am happy etc).

Once you choose the emotion you ideally would like to EXPERIENCE… Aha! You start your inner communication - not inner chat or dialogue - but your inner communication!

You start recognising where you feel that emotion, it is like switching your attention inward - and finding inside the memory or a spot that feels as though it does produce the desired emotion … and then EURIKA you come up with the decision to contact that person you met the other day who told you about that new company. The person suddenly announces that company is looking for an expert in your area of expertise! They put you in touch and - you get a brand new, better paid job - that is the influence of connectivity …

You don't really switch your mind off, you switch your feelings instead. Don't worry about the highly overrated eastern philosophy and the power of meditation if it doesn't work for you. Our ancestors were correct by saying to rest properly - you do not actually rest, you switch to a different activity. You want the energy flowing.

Before you start throwing stones at me and saying "but Olga, you told us we do not need to work hard in order to have what we want and now you say we need to work harder?"

I did not use the word work but the word 'activity'. Holidays, reading a book, taking your dog for a walk, checking in on your neighbour is an activity too.

Since we are overpowered with what we should do, rather than knowing what is the best for us (and all) to do next we need to re- learn about ourselves which activity supports our 'switching off rationale' and switching on our 'internal communication'. Bizarrely it is usually connected with some sort of interaction.

I had a lucky opportunity to observe one of the leading geniuses of this century at work. He really couldn't understand why it is that people would not accept a perfectly plausible and proven new theory of language accusation so easily. My suggestions went down the drain, partially because they were someone else's suggestions and he had no connection with that. Now here is an interesting aspect, he didn't stop trying to look for solution yet rather than concentrating on finding the solution he simply has acknowledged this fact and continues his research. Unsurprisingly for me and most amusingly for most, the solution came from a seemingly unrelated source, when the university he was about to give his next talk at asked him to explain what has made him to come up with such approach.

Here is what an ordinary human being calls synchronicity, and the correct term is 'connectivity'. The university suggestion was that bit of radiation to awake the comfortable innate use in him. Partially because it was not the right time in a sense that possibly now a group of scientists wanted a better opportunity to learn how languages are acquired. Hence the scientist's idea had the right time to come to the surface.

I also had to learn my own ways of working my seemingly at first innate ideas. I was completely stuck at one point during the writing of this book. No meditation, yoga classes, extreme sports or other extreme activities did it for me. I tried to meet others. We people have smart dialogues.

I told myself time after time that I have it inside me, it is about how I awaken it this time. Yes I've been enjoying my life again by watching movies, reading new books, meeting interesting people and yet it hit me that I've forgotten.

You own inner knowledge and an understanding. The true understanding of us, our inter-connectivity and the fact that all I need is inside me. I simply need to turn my attention inwards.

That's when I start 'learning' myself again. That's when I switched my rationale mind and simply analyzed what was it that I did that made me write my books so fast towards the end of them.

Especially my last book, which was mostly written during my trip to Japan! Mostly on the plane during my long flight hours. And it daunts me that whenever I travel my perception is open to new and unexpected experiences rather than trying to find a solution.

There I was, travelling to Rome. Something unusual happened to me. It was my first trip to Rome and I remembered how much I love surprises. There we were on a Valentine day 2012 in a new modern style restaurant with this 'molecular' style cuisine and I suddenly demanded for the waitress not to tell me what it is I am served. If you know the type of restaurant I am referring to you'll know what pride they take in explaining what the hell they are serving you and they really indulge in observing your surprised face - oh but that so doesn't taste like such and such.

I really felt for her, but it was about me. Not knowing what I was to be served had reminded me that only few days ago I understood what Plato meant with his shadows in a cave. In turn this led to a discussion with my darling, and it is his questions (because he couldn't understand my explanation) which has led me to progress with this book.

That's how my Valentine's surprise dinner gave me that charge I needed to awaken my inner knowledge, and continue writing this book.

With inner communication you simply need to re-learn your own knowledge of yourself. The best way is to observe yourself either by making mental notes or keeping a diary. Observing oneself is a key to a more fulfilling life and an opportunity to have richer experiences. As well as a surefire way to stay Mentally Healthy.

You forget that you are a spiritual being first of all, and that the body is something new to you. Just as a child takes time to learn to walk or to speak - you need to take time to see how your body influences your mind and vice versa. It is by learning those unique triggers that you have the opportunity of perpetum-mobile (the permanent engine) - what it means in real terms or in our spiritual language. That is the way we keep momentum going and that is our key to switching on and off that 'momentum'. Let's be upfront about it – at times it is simply being in the moment, staying still and simply experiencing being alive that is what we really want. And by learning your own key you will have that opportunity to dip in and out of life processes as you wish and at your desired speed.

The key is not permanent, for your body evolves (I don't like to use term- ageing here) it simply goes through changes that in turn affect you.

While I still insist and you know best that your mind is the source of power - I suggest you look at it this way. We are in a physical world and that in turn will influence us until we learn.

12

Thoughts

One of the main reasons for people staying in their circle of mental health issues seem to be the ability to possess multiple lasting self-destructive monologues.

Such monologues seem to be fueled by the constant stream of thoughts which are hardly controlled, if ever at all. Modern human beings do not realise that the thought processes we have are not always ours, nor do we realise that thought processes are something that need to be controlled.

Most people currently are quite the opposite, controlled by thoughts. Either their own or those of their partners and in most cases by the thoughts of whatever is 'floating' around. Partially due to our need to interact and connect with others and partially due to our exposure to the multiple streams of information directing our ways via advertising, newspapers, TV, movies, books we read, people we work for or people we work with, our children and even our animals.

As we are subjected to such streams of thoughts and we have no ability, nor even knowledge of the need to control our thoughts and how to block unwelcome thoughts. We really are 'floating' in our time.

That in turn results in many people seemingly working towards one goal yet miraculously achieving another goal. Such as accepting a job offer that simply came their way and then later realising that was not their ideal job. Such as getting married to a person, later on realising the person may be great yet it was either your parents or those surrounding you who wanted to see you married, without any concern for your personal needs and desires and priorities. Partially because you yourself do not know what they are, as you are not in control of your thoughts and you are constantly subjected to digesting thoughts of the others, random thoughts.

Let me give you an example. You are in a car with a friend, you are returning from a countryside break back into your city you both live in. Suddenly your friend proposes you stop at a particular restaurant. You are amazed and exclaiming "Wow, that is the restaurant I was just thinking about!"

Chances are your friend was contemplating possible locations for the next meal and after weighing several options has decided to pick that particular restaurant. You have picked up your friends thoughts without realising it, because you do not expect that you are a full-time *receiver* of wanted and unwanted thoughts floating around you.

The interesting effect is such that due to the *synchronicity* according to your understanding of life, you agree to go to the restaurant.

Should you return home alone and have a shower or simply lie in bed with no thoughts (rarely, yet let's presume for the purpose of the example) and you think "why did I think of that restaurant, I don't even like Italian kitchen". You became confused and since analyzing requires extra mental training, you simply drift in your thoughts towards next thoughts floating by and fell asleep soundly.

The other classic example is when you think of someone and then you meet the person or the person rings you. This one can be tricky. You simply pick up the thoughts of that person. Quite a different example to the commonly used 'thought of her/him and the person called'.

I was after a particular outfit in a fashionable boutique in London. The boutique belongs to a chain. While I normally go to their Marylebone branch, the circumstances turned such a way that I ended up in an alternative branch in Westbourne Grove. Simultaneously I thought of a friend who used to work for the Alaia brand in another boutique. Confused to why would I even think of her at that moment, I sent the thought away.

The boutique, did have the item but not in my size and they had to order it in. I was looking forward to making an extra trip the very next day to get the much desired outfit. My friend was on my mind again. I dismissed the thought. The next day I arrived, the driver with my order was late and I had to leave empty handed and very disappointed. While I am quite trained with my cause-effect-chain-reactions, I got grumpy and ended up shopping in another boutique getting another yet equally hot outfit (which just a week later, and rather conveniently I wore for Glyndebourne, the event I forgot I had to get a new outfit for!). Again, realising my situation, I still felt grumpy and decided not to come back to that shop. While you can happily discuss the childishness of the situation, there is a continuation to those events. A few days later, I received a phone call from the shop that they got my size in, feeling still grumpy towards them but excited the outfit was about to be mine at last, I confirmed that I could make it next day at around noon.

The next day I had an emergency and could only reach the shop by 3pm. As I enter the store, my friend who I was thinking about few times earlier stood right there, in a middle of the shop. Apparently she has left the Alaia brand and now works for this boutique. Coincidence? Possibly. Yet neither of us had felt the need right now to get in touch with each other, nor do we socialize on a regular basis. I've simply picked, subconsciously, familiar thought waves belonging to her, hence I thought of her.

A less obvious example would be, if you are in a shop and you've spotted something that got your attention, you've gone over, read the label and thought 'hmm, that looks interesting, I should try'. You end up purchasing it.

Without even realising that that item was advertised either on TV or in the press and your mind has scanned it and processed it due to your attention spam, should you be hungry for examples while reading the sports updates section. Since you were hungry, your mind dutifully scanned the pages you were reading for anything food related. You, meanwhile, based on the limitation towards what your conscious can accept had no clue that your mind has performed a trick on you.

While such influences seem to be harmless, they are not in fact.

There is what I call a PWS (pregnant woman syndrome). Ever noticed how if you yourself or someone in your family is pregnant, you start noticing how many other women are pregnant right now. It often happens to women who suspect they may be pregnant but not sure yet they do notice all the pregnant women around, suddenly. Just like that.

Such PWS I use to explain any spiraling effect on any thought you hold for longer than any other thoughts. For example, if you feel unfairly criticised at your work and on return to your home you get much needed support and reconfirmation on how wonderful you are, the thought stays re-playing itself in your mind.

Should you be looking for a new position and your first interview was unsuccessful, the first thought keeps re-accentuating and spirals out as a mini tsunami picking up on the similar thoughts of others. Before too long, you are sucked into the self-destructive thought patterns of yourself and those around you, without you knowing, understanding or realising that.

If more events reconfirm your current thought patterns, which let's be honest is more common than not, depression or other mental health illness is a sure thing in the near future. Because you are NOT strong enough to stop your thought patterns without the interference of a strong stimulus.

Sometimes for my clients, I am just that. A strong stimulus that can re-program their thought patterns. I don't advertise myself like that. Because we are not aware of how much self-destruction there is in our lives from an inability to stay connected with our own needs, desires and our own unique talents.

Or as it is popular to say nowadays: 'Your Life Purpose.'

Should you need some more information on that, I'd recommend you highly to read my previous book, *How To Be Selfish. And Other Uncomfortable Advice.*

It is a great book as it also has supportive exercises. Should you be deep in depression and feeling too weak to take control of your thoughts without a major intervention please seek help from a psychiatrist. Should you feel you are healthy and you have no chances of mental health illnesses (at least you think so) yet you seemingly live in circles and no matter what you do you always end up in a similar situations (especially in relationships with other people) get a personal development coach. Just the presence of another human being who has your interests at heart can produce the much-needed starting point *miracle*.

When it comes to relationships with other people. It is not their problem you pick up their thoughts. In order to stay clear of anyone's influence, you need to learn to quiet your mind and block yourself from any sources of information and any contact with others for a short period of time.

Just ten minutes a day will do you more good than a long break on an uninhabited island. Learning to control has nothing to do with isolation, as you need to learn to have your switch turned on and off whenever you are next to others! Quite the opposite, controlling thoughts is only one of the central parts of how to learn to communicate with others clearly.

Next time you feel angry or sad, consider whether these thoughts are really yours.

Instead of the ending...

Are you ill? Am I ill? Are we ill? Or is the whole society ill?

You decide.

Yet it's time to stop blaming others, it's time to stop playing games with others. It's time to abandon living the lives of others.

It is time to start living your own life fully.

Stop awaking guilt in your children to make them do stuff for you. Stop making your parents responsible for your poor upbringing or lack of toys.

It is now the time to turn inward and learn about yourself and your opportunities. You always have a choice. If you don't, you overlooked other options. But stop blaming others for your issues and for your depressions, your anxieties and whatnot.

If you can't control your own life, you are only fooling yourself into believing you can control lives of others.

In fact the more you believe so, the more delusional and mentally sick you become. No one owns anyone, apart from the pure and simple recognition that each is a fellow human.

There is no emotional debt. There is no obligation for anyone to provide for you.

There is an urgent need to start understanding yourself and start living your own life.

Note: People are not angry, unless something important is happening to them. They may be hurt, or afraid, or going through something very difficult for them. Anger can be their defence mechanism.

Also by this Author

Increase Your Confidence in One Day

How to be Selfish (And other uncomfortable advice)

'*Increase your Confidence in One Day*' explores the true meaning of confidence, and helps readers to unlock their potential, release the fears that are holding them back and make real life changes that will have a strong and lasting effect.

In today's competitive marketplace, confidence is the single most important quality you can have. Confidence can unlock hidden potential and help you be the best you can be in all areas of your life.

'Increase your Confidence in One Day' has already been a life-changing read for thousands of people across the world. Here is what one reader has to say:

"Olga has an amazing talent for change. Whether the change you are looking for is a transformation in the way you manage a company, or a more personal relationship-oriented goal, Olga can deliver. This book is quite inspiring — it's an overused cliché to say that it will change your life, but it just might"

— DR ALEX CLARK
Lecturer in Logic and Linguistics
Department of Philosophy
King's College London

'*How to be Selfish*' explores the common traps that people fall into trying to please others or to fit in, and asks some challenging questions about our place in society, gender roles, relationships and money. It teaches a new, liberating way of life where selfishness is no longer viewed as a negative trait. The book is released in two versions, a standard version and an X-rated version which includes an additional chapter on sex and gender.

http://amzn.to/19shdXD
www.OlgaLevancuka.com
www.SkinnyRichCoach.com

Made in the USA
Charleston, SC
13 October 2013